THE NIGHT THE GIANT ROLLED OVER

Among other books by Jerry Jenkins

Sammy Tippit: God's Love in Action
Bad Henry (with Hank Aaron)
The Gingerbread Man (with Pat Williams)
The Story of Dick Motta
Paul Anderson: The World's Strongest Man
Three Behind the Curtain
Home Where I Belong (with B. J. Thomas)
Running for Jesus (with Madeline Manning Jackson)
Sweetness (with Walter Payton)
The Luis Palau Story
The Margo Mystery Series
  Margo
  Karlyn
  Hilary
  Paige

THE NIGHT THE GIANT ROLLED OVER

Jerry Jenkins

WORD BOOKS
PUBLISHER
WACO, TEXAS

ISBN 0-8499-0111-1
Library of Congress catalog card number: 80-54549
Printed in the United States of America

To
Ed and Nancy Robinson
and
Dennis and Nancy Stuessi
who epitomize the joy of selfless service

Contents

The Sowers

First Reports

THE SOWERS, THE FLIERS, AND THE JUNGLE

You wouldn't want to live there. In fact, it's not even a nice place to visit.

Remote is the kindest term for Irian Jaya (EER-ee-an-JAH-ya), the most easterly province of the Indonesian archipelago that occupies the western half of the island of New Guinea.

Other than in the immediate vicinity of the larger towns, there are no roads in Irian and all transportation to the interior is by air or water. The primary means of communication is by radio provided by Mission Aviation Fellowship, which operates its largest base at the Sentani (sen-TAH-nee) Airport and serves small mountain airstrips built by missionaries.

Sentani lies on the northern coast of Irian and on a flat world map is located north of Australia and at the end of a straight line running from Los Angeles through Hawaii.

Just 25 miles east is Jayapura (jie-ua-PUR-ah), seat of the provincial governor. The city boasts automotive traffic, stores, shops, restaurants, and even some long distance telephones. But just over the mountains south of Sentani live the most primitive people on earth. Officially considered technically developed to the level of the New Stone Age, these near-pygmies of Melanesian stock wear almost no clothes and keep warm at night by either sleeping near small fires or smearing their bodies with pig fat.

Their huts are rudimentary. They have no cooking or eating utensils, roasting their limited foodstuffs on an open flame or in coals. Cannibalism is still evident in some parts. From the air, this area appears to be 99 percent foliage on steep mountainsides, broken up only by huge winding rivers and occasional clearings for tiny villages and food gardens. Emergency landing areas are all but nonexistent.

There's an element of natural beauty in Irian Jaya, but the pleasant memories my wife and I have of our visit are of the men and women who are there because that is where God wants them.

They make no big deal of it. Each must have had his or her own times of doubt and reconsidering along the way, but the mature missionary or pilot or mechanic or technician has long since put behind him the second thoughts and soul-searching and the longing for an air-conditioned, bug free home where the heat and humidity don't force people to bed soon after sundown.

For the most part we met people who have either decided not to dwell on the inconvenience of mission field life, or who once genuinely dealt with it and have rendered it a nonissue. These are not special saints, but they are people to whom luxury is irrelevant and who don't cry over its absence.

Who are these people and how does one tell their story? They are united in their mission—to serve God by sharing Christ with the primitive Irian nationals—but they serve different mission boards and are stationed at bases miles from each other. And even those who serve together come from incredibly diverse backgrounds.

Other than with a string of anecdotes and profiles, a book about such people would be impossible unless there were some common denominator, some adhesive element or event which ties them all together.

We found both. For years, Mission Aviation Fellowship has provided the missions in the area with air transportation and radio communication that makes the eclectic Irian missionaries one big happy family.

For decades the MAF pilots have been the missionaries' only contact with civilization and with each other. When supplies, medicine, food, personnel, messages, or mail had to be sent or received, MAF was the instrument. The thousands upon thousands of hours of flying, dangerous as it is, may have become routine to the veteran pilots at times. But it was this routine that stocked such a storehouse of safety-conscious expertise that when the tragedy to end all tragedies struck at 4:20 A.M. June 25, 1976, MAF and the missionaries it served were able to cope heroically.

The massive earthquake, the event that tested and proved the family, saw the missionaries (via MAF) provide relief, shelter, food, and medical assistance. They averted even more destruction and chaos by serving as liaison between national and international relief organizations and task forces. And they increased their own credibility with the Indonesian government and the nationals.

To keep up with the unbelievable demands for food and supplies in the months following the quake, MAF was forced to beef up its inventory with more and better planes and helicopters. By using these more sophisticated and expensive machines to their fullest efficiency, MAF proved their contention that such equipment could change the face of missions in the area.

Many of the planes pressed into action by the tragedy are still operating, carrying supplies and personnel into areas never before open to the Christian message. And it all stemmed from that horrifying morning one June day when the giant who sleeps under the earth—whose occasional stirring had caused annoying ground tremors for centuries—finally rolled over and sent the mountains crashing into the valleys.

MAF, the missionaries it serves, the nationals, and all of Irian Jaya would never be the same. Using certain MAF people who happened to be in the right place at the right time and with the earthquake as the focal point, here is the true story from those who were there.

The Giant Rolls Over

June 24–25, 1976

The world is shaken more than two thousand times a day by the shifting or crashing together of mobile, fifty-mile-thick crustal plates that cover the surface of the globe. Only the most sensitive seismographs can detect as many as five percent of these, but at least a dozen times a year violent quakes rattle the complete depths of these plates and snap the topography like a crack-the-whip game.

Indonesia is a prime spot for tremors and significant earthquakes because it is located where the crustal plates beneath the ocean thrust under land plates. But "significant" is a minor league word for the quake that ripped through Irian Jaya one fateful pre-dawn Saturday in 1976.

June 24 was one of the blackest nights anyone could remember, but nothing in the climate or atmosphere forewarned of danger. It was cool in the mountains, as usual—good sleeping weather. On the coast it was hot and clammy, as usual. Missionaries and mission pilots had had a busy day. People happy in their work and at peace in their spirits sleep well.

These were exciting days in mission work in Irian Jaya; there were new people and new techniques and new equipment. But for the most part, it was business as usual. A ton of duties and chores loaded everyone's list for the next morning. And there was that sense of urgency to "sleep fast, because dawn comes early no matter when you hit the pillow."

Nearly everyone was asleep by 9:30 P.M., and certainly everyone was by 11:00. Acclimated, tired, challenged, motivated, they slept soundly, heavily. Mothers conditioned to keep one slice of their minds awake to the needs of their children would have awakened to a cry, but not to a slight tremor so common to the area, and certainly not to animal noises which had long since become just another part of the background.

Scientists are hard pressed to know exactly when the geological changes occur underground that result in violent chaos on the surface. They do know that a few hours before an up-top manifestation of the shifting and churning thousands of feet below, animals are aware of noises or movement humans do not detect.

In Irian Jaya, a couple of hours after midnight, June 25, 1976, reptiles skittered here and there. Pigs rooted and grunted, but not even the nationals noticed. There may have been some minor tremors by 3:00 A.M. A swarm of undetectable foreshocks built up quickly and suddenly ceased.

The tribespeople in the mountains stirred just before 4:00 A.M. and started fires outside their huts. Their animals were noisier than usual, sensing the vibrations and smelling the rare radon gas scientists say is released by the seismic pressure that squeezes moisture from rock and raises nearby water levels before an eruption of the earth. The creatures may have even sensed changes in electrical fields as the rock became more resistant to currents.

The area became deathly still. How long the foreshocks lasted or how long the silence hung before the rupture of the fault, no one knows. Deep below the ground, something gave way. At precisely 4:20 A.M., Saturday, June 25, 1976, the whip cracked, the earth split, the ground shook, the topsoil tore away from the steep mountainsides, and a tremor lasting a full eight minutes and measuring between 7.1 and 7.8 on the Richter scale changed the complexion of 2,000 square miles of the central mountain range in the Oskibil, Okbap, and Kurima districts of the Jayawijaya Regency, Irian Jaya, Indonesia.

For the record, the epicenter was 140° 29′ E, 04° 30′ S, near the eastern extremity of the geographic center of the island, approximately 37 miles from the Papua New Guinea border. More than 15,000 people live in the area in small, self-contained villages close to their food gardens. They represent an estimated 100,000 tribal inhabitants of the most rugged populated area in the world who have never made friendly contact with the outside.

Tons of earth and rocks and water thundered down the mountains, gathering trees and gardens and even whole villages as they snowballed into the valleys and the Bime River. Instant landslides caused natural dams that immediately formed huge lakes at high levels that would suddenly break loose and cause more havoc. An area one hundred miles long and twenty miles wide was stripped of 80 percent of its vegetation in minutes. And the aftershocks, two within the next hour, caused Richter readings of as high as 5.0 each, more intense than many single earthquakes in the world.

The fragile, primitive huts of the tribespeople tumbled into their own fires or were swept down the mountains. Four entire villages in the Bime area were washed away, resulting in eighty-three deaths. More than eight hundred were eventually reported dead, a remarkably small toll, attributable to low population density and to the fact that the tribespeople were already up before the quake and were able to scramble to higher ground as their belongings were swept away.

The Sowers

THE COLES
June 24–25, 1976

Unevangelized Fields Mission had many missionaries in the area. Dave and Dolly Brumagin and their children, Rick (then 13) and Karen (11), were building a small house near a landing strip at Eipomek where they planned to open a mission base. They had been in language study at Nalca for three months after having spent about a year at Mulia. They settled down for the night of June 24 in a small tent some hundred or so feet from another smaller tent with just one occupant.

He was Dave Cole, a lifetime veteran of the Irian Jaya mission field. He and his wife, Dina, had been serving since 1958, living among the Dani tribespeople, learning their language, helping them survive, and sharing Christ with them without trying to westernize them. Dave is an earthy man who enjoys physical labor and seeing things come together. He was helping build the Brumagins' new house, and while he didn't enjoy sleeping in a tent several minutes flying time from Dina and their house at Bime, it was not a new experience for him.

Nor was it for Dina, back at Bime. A handsome, unpretentious, straightforward woman whose soft eyes and smile belie a fierce protectiveness of the people she ministers to, she had endured nights alone in the bush before. Self-assured and self-sufficient in the practical things of life, she was safe enough.

15

Her househelpers were within earshot. The doors could be locked if she felt it necessary. The Coles' house in the mountains was a roomy, frame affair on pilings, and she had acquired just enough niceties to make the place homey in more than eighteen years on the field. It would hardly serve as a vacation spot for westerners, but it was more than adequate for Dina and Dave, who had raised their two children in Irian.

The Coles are the "parent" missionaries of the area. Quick to give God the credit for any strides they have made with the tribespeople, they are doing the work the old way, knowing the minds of the people. Unevangelized Fields Mission Field Leader Dave Scovill often sought the Coles' counsel before making decisions regarding the local nationals and UFM's work among them.

In June 1976, after serving several terms under UFM in other areas of Irian, Dave and Dina Cole had been working in Bime for more than a year. The work had begun slowly as they struggled to break down the tribespeople's fear and penetrate their superstition-oriented society. By now many of the locals had become Christians and loved the Coles as well as their Lord. Some of them called Dave and Dina father and mother. The Coles' sons, Larry and Bruce, had numerous friends among the nationals.

Before going to bed the night before the earthquake, Dina busied herself preparing her shelves for cleaning the next day. The boys had gone back to school, and with Dave helping the Brumagins at Eipomek, Dina devoted her indoor evening time to this project. Ironically, she left her dishes on the counter and table so they'd be out of the way for the next day's scrub-down of the shelves. It was those dishes rattling, then crashing to the floor, that awakened her at 4:20 A.M.

She'd been awakened by tremors before. Sometimes they were big enough to make her consider hustling the family outside to protect against injury should the house break up. But usually a tremor simply rocked the house gently, waking everyone for a breath-catching pause to see if that was all, and then letting them cautiously fall back to sleep.

This shaking quake left no doubt in Dina's mind that there would be no more sleeping. Her house was being ripped from the bottom up; dishes were shattering, doors flying open, glass breaking, floors tilting this way and that. *This is the real thing,* she thought. She bolted from her bed and scrambled beneath it.

At Eipomek, several miles away, Dave Cole had been asleep in his tent—his sleeping bag resting on a thin bamboo mat—as close to the ground as he could be. A sudden jolt made the earth billow under and past him like an ocean wave. He sat straight up. It was as if some monstrous force had grabbed the plot of ground his tent lay on and whipped it into the air like you would straighten a blanket while making a bed. The wave came back with another violent snap, and Dave tried to peer out. Pitch black.

He heard landslides and the frightened Danis yelling from below, in characteristic dread fear in the face of natural calamity. Hollering over to the Brumagin tent Dave found that they were all right and then realized that there was nothing he could do until dawn. He climbed back into his sleeping bag, not to sleep but to ride out the aftershocks which just kept coming and coming.

He was on a free roller-coaster ride in the middle of nowhere, sharply aware that a huge landslide could even reach his tent but also that there was really nothing to do and nowhere to go. He'd been through a lot in his years on the field with Dina and the boys, and he wasn't going to panic now. If this was his time to go, then this was his time.

In Bime, Dina Cole's house kept rocking and seemed to be turning. The noises grew louder and she tried to identify each as she was thrown from side to side under the bed. One unmistakable sound, though she had never heard a big one before, was a landslide. Rumbling, tumbling, thundering down the mountains near the airstrip and her small outpost, the clamor seemed endless. Even so, she knew it had just begun only an instant before.

She believes God told her—though not audibly—to get out from under the bed. Even after having been awake for several seconds her eyes would not adjust to the pitch. As she crawled out she cut her feet and elbow on glass from some broken oil lamps. Dazed, she limped out of the bedroom and *uphill* to the back door. It didn't compute. The floors had been flat and square, made as tight and true as possible in the middle of nowhere by missionary craftsmen with years of experience. *Why is the floor at such an angle now? What must the room look like?*

Dina groped for a flashlight, but her belongings were so topsy-turvy she could hardly recognize the objects she did put her hands on. Still she saw nothing in the blackness. She reached the back door and grabbed Dave's jacket to cover her nightgown. The door was jammed shut. Healthy and strong as she was, she couldn't budge it. She needed something to wear on her feet. Meanwhile, the confusing noises continued.

She started at the sound of calm voices in the next room, before realizing she was hearing—over the sound of her pounding heart—a radio that had banged to the floor and turned itself on. From upstairs came another eerie sound. She recognized that as their record player just turning and whining in the brief pauses between the thunderous roars of onrushing debris and falling trees.

Dina Cole was not one to panic, but she began to think of the irony of dying in her own house, unable to open her own door, wearing her husband's jacket and no shoes, walking blind in the darkness and fearing everything that went bump in the night—including the night itself.

Presently she pulled herself together and attempted to move into the living room. The way was blocked by the stairway which seemed to hold everything that had once been upstairs. *Got to get some shoes on and get out of the house,* she told herself.

Rubble blocked the front door. Digging through it, Dina found a right and a left tennis shoe her sons had left for the local people. They were different pairs, she would discover later, but she worked them on anyway.

Image-consciousness was not part of her missionary mentality, but Dina was strangely grateful that she did not have to see herself, let alone be seen, in that getup. Had the house fallen on her in that instant, she'd have died wearing one article of clothing from each of the men in her life.

As she became completely conscious, Dina was suddenly aware of how cold she was, and of the superficial cuts she had sustained. Her eye was tender and sensitive and she accurately predicted that it would blacken—but from what, she did not know.

She was unaware that her house had dropped approximately seven feet when several of the supporting pillars came up through the floor. One—she would discover later—blasted right through her bed and would have killed her had she remained under it. The whole shifting, swaying structure had slid some ten feet. Her front door was now at ground level.

Dina felt for the porch and realized it was gone. She was afraid to jump, thinking that without the porch she would be several feet off the ground. All she could feel beyond the doorway were scrap boards and loose material, but she knew she had to get out. Moving gingerly with short steps, and sometimes crawling, she made it out of the house, calling for her househelper who was usually just minutes away.

There was no response.

THE BRUMAGINS
June 25, 1976

Dave and Dolly Brumagin knew immediately that the jet-enginelike roar and the violent rocking of the earth beneath them meant earthquake. As they and their children, Rick and Karen, awoke at the same moment, that's the one word they shouted in unison.

It seemed that the entire mountain range was shaking like a dried leaf in the wind. They froze in terror at the sound of giant rocks ripping up the huge trees as they blasted down the mountainsides. Their tent, a hundred feet from Dave Cole's, was, like his, positioned in a fairly open spot. But in the blackness, as the earth shook them to the bone, it seemed as if the landslides would overtake them any second and they would be crushed. Dolly clicked on her flashlight.

Young Rick tried to get to his feet. But anyone who has ever experienced even a tiny tremor knows that strange feeling that you have no foundation. Your equilibrium is based on solid ground and when that is shifting, you feel lost in space, out of whack, unbalanced. For Rick it was even worse, for this was no tremor. At Eipomek, the Brumagins were in the epicenter of one of history's most violent earthquakes [despite the low death toll, it ranks among the five worst ever in total disfiguration of nature], the ground hurling them up and down, and Rick could

20

get only halfway up before being driven to his knees.

Dolly Brumagin, a little-girl-appearing woman who could pass for ten years younger than she is, feared for her children's lives and ordered them to lie still as she and Dave began to pray. Within a few seconds after having been awakened she had had more than enough. The rumbling and the deafening roar continued and the landslides intensified. The shocks banging back and forth under them threw first Dave and Dolly up into the air and then as they rocked back down, the children were pushed up. They bobbed up and down for several minutes as if on a mad Trampoline.

"Oh no, oh no, oh no, oh no!" Dolly cried every time the earth moved. Dave tried to calm her and answered Dave Cole's call to assure him that their family was all right. But in the darkness he wondered if they would survive. It was a hundred times worse than they would have even dreamed, had they ever thought they would endure an earthquake.

Directly behind the Brumagins' tent, which was situated on a little knoll, was a larger hill—a garden area—and behind that a small valley and creek. On beyond was a big cliff where most of the landslide was taking place. Dave counted on the size of that valley and the distance between them and the cliff to keep them from being flattened, but the longer the roaring and sliding continued, the less optimistic he was.

Dolly was nearly beside herself with panic and doesn't remember as much about what she said or did as her family does. The kids were too terrified to cry. While Dolly may wish she had been more brave or resourceful, there was nothing she could have done for almost an hour because of the darkness and the helpless knowledge that, as flimsy as a tent would be against a landslide, there was no better shelter.

There was nowhere to go, nothing to do. When that is the case you either resign yourself to your fate—as Dave Cole was doing a hundred feet away—or you worry yourself sick. Which is what Dolly did.

The Fliers

JERRY REEDER
June 25, 1976

The earthquake had rocked pilot Jerry Reeder and his family in
their beds for about a minute at 4:20 A.M., as it had everyone
else at Mission Aviation Fellowship's Irian headquarters base in
Sentani. It did not force them outside, but nearly everyone let
that possibility cross his mind when the shaking lasted so long.
When it finally stopped and the dogs stopped barking, everyone
went back to sleep.

At 6:15 A.M., Jerry would sit in his Cessna 185 on the
runway, ready to take off for Eipomek for a makeup flight
occasioned by the previous week's bad weather. He would turn
on his radio to get a weather report from the interior and just
listen for the first ten minutes, fascinated by a report from
Okbap.

He would learn that the one-minute rock that had awakened
the Sentani compound had not been just a tremor after all. And
he would find himself in the middle of all the radio traffic and
calls for aid. At age thirty-eight he would be busier than ever in
his life.

Indeed he would become the pivot man in the crisis, proving
himself the perfect, though reluctant, choice.

JERRY REEDER
1951–1959

Jerry Reeder had been an unlikely candidate for the mission field since day one. Someone planning to build a missionary probably wouldn't start with Jerry Reeder parts. A medium-sized, dark haired, shy man, he doesn't fit any of the stereotypes of one who decides to live for God in some remote corner of the world. He doesn't come from a long line of preachers or missionaries. He's not even a second-generation Christian. Born the son of an International Business Machines machinist in Endicott, New York, Jerry was an only child, a keep-out-of-trouble kid, and—by his own admission—"just kind of a nobody."

The son of the pastor of a small local church took an interest in the boys in Jerry's neighborhood, and when Jerry was thirteen he finally accepted the boy's invitation to attend an evangelistic meeting. There he received Christ, but it would be a half dozen years before his life would significantly change.

Despite his new faith, he found it hard to apply himself at school. Except for subjects he really liked, such as electronics lab or something similar, Jerry struggled along on academic probation, barely passing. He hardly had the will to live, let alone concentrate.

After attending a local community college for training in

electrical technology, Jerry moved away from home to a rooming house in Poughkeepsie, New York, and—following in his father's footsteps—began working for IBM.

Jerry recalls those early days on his own as a time when he was in a "cold Christian limbo. I wasn't really living the Christian life, but I wasn't turned off to it either. I could come right up to its fire and warm myself in the fellowship at church, but I was unproductive. I didn't go the other way, carousing in bars or anything, but I felt as if I was in some sort of a twilight zone, not committing myself either way."

Jerry's otherwise lonely evenings were spent cruising around town, hopping from diner to diner looking for friends from church or work—someone, anyone to talk to.

Bud Williams, a friend from church who would later become his brother-in-law, told Jerry he could stop in and see him anytime. Jerry took him up on it two or three times a week, and Bud always gave him a spiritual kick in the pants, encouraging him to read Scripture regularly and getting him thinking about what he might do for the Lord. Bud seemed to have his own life mapped out and was very concerned about walking with and for the Lord. It got Jerry thinking about himself, and the more he read the Bible the more convinced he became that his conversion six years before had been the genuine article. And the more he read, the more he wanted to serve Christ.

One night while Bud was reading something to Jerry from the Bible, he suddenly looked up and said, "Maybe God is calling you to be a missionary." It was just a suggestion—something to think about—but it hit Jerry like a clap of thunder. The concept of possibly going into full-time service for God had been planted.

Jerry began to think long and hard about his future. He was moving up fast at IBM. He enjoyed a lot of privileges and had everything any aspiring electrical technician could want. He was placed in some newly developed departments and became head technician over fourteen workers, yet somehow he was restless. He wondered what his life would be like if he stayed on his current course.

He saw himself reaching retirement age and sitting in a rocking chair surveying what he had done over the previous forty-five years. *How will I feel about what I accomplish if I stay on this path?*

All things being equal, he knew he'd climb the technical, social, and financial ladders at IBM, and maybe he would even wind up with a patent or two to his name through the company. *But what will little-known and not-long-remembered Jerry Reeder really be known for?*

"That's when I realized that it would be gone, poof! Just like that. Still projecting myself into the rocking chair at the end of my working life, I wondered how I could alter my path now so that when I really reached that point, I would be able to look back with more of a sense of accomplishment and satisfaction— not for my fame or ego, but just to know that I had done something worthwhile. Then it dawned on me. I would have to be in full-time service for the Lord, anywhere that I could be involved in winning souls for His kingdom. That way, all through eternity I would meet people I might have had a hand in leading to Christ. I thought, *Now that's satisfying!*"

But it was also frustrating. He had a skill, a specialty. And the only full-time service he could think of was pastoring and missionary work. He knew he was not the pastor type, and "I couldn't see myself walking around in a pith helmet and riding in a Land-Rover either." Full-time Christian service appeared to be a dead end, but still it played on his mind. He knew he would only be fully satisfied at the end of a life of service to Christ.

On another of his nightly jaunts through town he snacked with Don Jackson, a friend from church, who offhandedly mentioned that the Moody Bible Institute of Chicago had a training program for missionary radio technicians. "I thought, *Hey, maybe that's something I can do.*" He wrote for the catalog, but when he read the description of the course, he realized it was similar to the training he had already received. But something else caught his eye: the mission aviation program. "I had never thought of that before, so I figured, *Maybe I'll try this door.*" Early in the summer of 1959 he joined twenty-three other applicants in a week-long course, from which Moody would choose twelve to enter the fall semester for the four-year aviation program. Jerry made the grade: "I had tried the door, and to my horror, it had opened."

Now twenty-one, Jerry returned to work in New York and told his boss he would be quitting in the fall to go to school. The first two years of the course involved classroom work at the downtown Chicago campus of the Institute, and the final two years were held at the old Moody Wooddale Airport in the suburbs. Jerry returned to New York during the summers of his first two years and worked in the product development lab at IBM at his old salary. The third year was devoted to mechanics at the airport, and when he began the last year—devoted to a heavy concentration of flying—he brought back with him the new Ethel Reeder, Bud Williams' sister.

JERRY REEDER
1962-1964

By December of 1962, Jerry Reeder had found himself again having trouble applying himself to his work. His grade school and high school problems were repeating themselves at the Moody Flight School, and he didn't know why. Surely he couldn't blame an unstable home life. In fact, his mother had become a Christian, and she and Jerry had been baptized the same day.

"I think I had just lost sight of my goal," he says. When it came time to take the practical flight test early in December, he failed. That wasn't unusual. The majority of such tests are failed the first time, but it became the last straw for Jerry's flight instructor. He had been forming a bad impression of Jerry, and as he had served a four-year term in Peru with JAARS (Jungle Aviation and Radio Service) himself, he expected a lot from his students. He called Jerry in.

Jerry knew, of course, that he had failed his first flight test, but he fully expected to be taking it again shortly, like all the others who had failed the first time. He was prepared for a pep talk, and maybe even a little Dutch uncle routine, but he was not prepared for all he heard from his instructor.

"From what I know of the mission field, Jerry—and I was there four years, as you know—and from what I know of you,

you don't have a ghost of a chance of making it. I'm recommending that you be dropped from the course."

If the instructor thought Jerry was just a rebel who would react like a tough guy and shake it off, he too was surprised. Jerry broke down and wept. "Listen," the instructor said, "I can put in a quick call to JAARS and maybe get you in as a radio man."

"I don't want to be a radio man," Jerry said, finally settling the matter in his mind and verbalizing his deepest wish for the first time. "I want to be a pilot." As he left the office he realized that he had made a big decision. He had reestablished his goal and he felt spiritually high. It was to be a turning point in his life. The other personnel at the airport sensed his disappointment and yet his commitment. He wasn't sure they could or would help him, but he knew he finally had his sights back on the original goal. He would become a pilot.

The chief flight instructor was the first to offer help. Dirk Van Dam, who still serves as director at the new Moody flight school in Elizabethton, Tennessee, offered to tutor Jerry after hours. "I'd like to help you, if you're interested." Jerry accepted, and soon another plum was dropped into his lap. Paul Wertheimer, the airport manager, asked Jerry if he thought he could install radios in the Moody planes in exchange for flight time in the training Cessnas.

Within hours of having been kicked out of the course, Jerry had access to the Moody planes and the best instructor, plus a job. He went back and passed the commercial license test, and during the last semester, while his former classmates were working on their instrument ratings in the course, he worked on his through Dirk. While he did not graduate, he finished at the same pace and earned the same tickets (licenses) as his classmates.

Then it was back to Buffalo so Ethel could finish the nurses' training she had interrupted to marry him. As they neared the city limits after the long drive from Chicago, Jerry kidded her,

"There'll probably be a big free-for-all in Buffalo, maybe even a riot when word gets around that I'm available for hire."

Nothing could have been farther from the truth. Jerry and Ethel Reeder spent the last of their meager funds for the first month's rent on an apartment and a week's groceries. Then it was job-hunting time.

For several days, Jerry looked for work at the local airports starting from the biggest—Buffalo Aeronautical—and working his way down to the one-runway-in-a-cow-pasture types. He never got to first base. He was new in the field, but he had fully expected to land at least some sort of flight instructing job somewhere. Finally resigning himself to falling back temporarily on his solid electronics history, he knocked on the doors of the major firms in the area—Westinghouse, General Electric, etc. Nothing.

I can always pump gas, he figured. As the bills began to roll in and the food ran low, Jerry visited fourteen gas stations in one day with no luck. He wasn't sure where to turn. He rummaged around in the attic of their apartment and came up with some old milk bottles worth enough in deposits for a loaf of bread.

Jerry had hoped to find something that would pay in the neighborhood of three dollars an hour, but at this point he was willing to take anything just to get some food on the table and a little pride back. He wanted to support his wife and get some practical aviation training so he could be ready when his big opportunity came. Surely the Lord wouldn't have led him to four years in Chicago for nothing. He was willing to take something else in the meantime, but something else didn't seem to be willing to take him.

His pastor, the Reverend Dale Fisher of the Calvary Baptist Church in Buffalo, phoned one night. "I need some new brake linings installed in my car," he said. "Is that a kind of work you can handle?" It earned Jerry sixteen dollars and a few more days. He had long since lost count of the number of places he had looked for a job. He and Ethel were learning tough lessons in humility, patience, prayer, and faith.

Meanwhile, his kind pastor was working in his behalf. To a church member who owned a fleet of dump trucks he dropped the word that Jerry was looking for work.

"Can you drive a dump truck?" the man asked.

"I don't know," Jerry said.

"Do you know the city?"

"I have a phone book and a map—"

"Bring your phone book and map and report here tomorrow morning."

Jerry drove truck for three months at $3.30 an hour until the day he noticed a grey Chrysler following him into the lot. Ignoring it, he jumped up on the trailer and began to unload.

"Lemme see your book, son," the man from the Chrysler said.

"What book is that?"

"Your union book."

"I don't have one."

"Then you'd better tell your boss you won't be coming in to work tomorrow."

Jerry asked how much union dues were and whether he could pay a little each week. The answer was no: "It was strictly cash and I was out of work again."

He finally badgered his way into a job as a mechanic's helper at Buffalo Aeronautical, but the job paid only $1.50 an hour and was temporary at best. He would work one week and be laid off the next. He and Ethel learned to live on very little—excellent training for the future.

A small company—the Prior Aviation Service—opened in one of the bays near where Jerry worked. They had just five planes and employed part-time pilots, but Jerry figured it was worth a try to see if they needed any full-time help.

By now it was the winter of 1963. Jerry was anxious to land something solid so he could work steadily to gain experience while Ethel completed her final year and a half of training. Then he hoped to catch on with a missionary aviation organization.

He put on a suit and tie and an overcoat and visited the Prior Aviation Service. It consisted of just a secretary and Jack Prior himself. As Jerry walked through the door, he brushed against it and a streak of wet white paint transferred itself to his topcoat. As he entered Prior's office, he grumbled, "Who's the idiot who painted that door and forgot to put up a sign?"

"Oh, did my sign blow away?" Prior asked. He went to a back room, painted himself a new sign, and applied it. Returning, he said, "Now what was it you wanted to see me about?"

Jerry's timing was perfect. Prior had taken his complaint good-naturedly and hired him at $2.00 an hour to be chief mechanic, flight instructor, charter pilot, floor sweeper, and whatever else he could find to do. "It's not much money," Prior told him, "but you'll get all the experience you want."

For the next eighteen months, Jerry and Ethel thought and prayed about Irian Jaya, the mission field Jerry had learned about at Moody when a missionary pilot—Bob Johansen—came to a class and showed his slides. He and Ethel felt God was leading them there, and when Jerry applied at MAF, he was told by personnel director Don Berry to continue getting experience for as long as possible and to "contact us again when your wife's training is finished." Jerry was amazed at himself for having had the audacity to even apply to "what I thought was the cream of the mission aviation outfits after having flunked out of Moody's flight training program. I'm sure MAF took me only on the personal recommendations of Dirk Van Dam and Paul Robinson (founder of the program). (Robinson told Reeder years later that he felt Jerry should never have been dropped from the course.)

By the end of 1964, the Reeders had been accepted as candidates for the mission field through Mission Aviation Fellowship, in Fullerton, California. "We want to know if you feel called to any particular field before we tell you what we have in mind," the Reeders were told.

"Irian Jaya," Jerry said.

"That's exactly where we were thinking."

Candidacy involved work in the hangar, some flying, and several orientation classes. After a year and a half of deputation work and another couple of months of intensive orientation (which included advanced field-condition flying in California), the Reeders—including baby Claude born in August 1965—were finally shipped to Irian Jaya in July 1966.

Jerry's life of meaningful work that would allow him to rock his retirement away in peace and satisfaction was about to begin. Would he have changed his life's course and invested all his time and energy and miles if he had known it could all end within six months?

•

JERRY REEDER
1966–1967

Except for the brief stopovers en route, Indonesia was the first foreign country Jerry Reeder had ever visited. In 1966, the capital city of Djakarta (the *D* has since been dropped)—still a whole day's flight from the MAF compound at Sentani—was wallowing in the pits of economic depression. It was bad enough that the town was muggy and the heat oppressive, but the 24-hour-a-day stench of smoke, auto exhaust, and sewage seemed to become part of one's clothing and person. Even the cold showers couldn't wash it away.

President Suharto tried to keep order with tanks and armored personnel carriers rumbling through the lonely streets. Garbage rotted everywhere; this once and future city of mass traffic jams and crowds of humanity had ground to a halt. There were only a few traffic lights in the entire city, but now their lenses dangled; their bulbs had been stolen.

When the Reeders arrived in Sentani and were shown the city of Jayapura to the east where they could purchase supplies, they were met by the same scenes as in Jakarta. Stores were nearly empty, their owners standing idly in the doorways. One shop had no merchandise left except a few light bulbs and a stark row of rubber duckies on a dusty shelf. Jerry figured that this must be what all foreign countries were like.

Sentani was a world unto itself. The dozen or so mostly young families of MAF personnel live in a self-contained community and make up the staff of administrators who double as pilots, pilots who double as administrators, mechanics, radio technicians, and wives and children. While they enjoy indoor plumbing, electricity, and at least cold running water, these people share their lives with millions of bugs, temperatures in the hundreds, hardly any privacy, and the constant fear that the radio might bring airplane news that no one wants to hear.

Jerry and his quiet wife knew they would face inconveniences and that their quarters would not be as nice as even a modest place in the United States. For this first term they would roll with the punches, take life as it came, and not complain.

It would be nearly four years later, when they would return to the States for their first furlough, that this huge difference in lifestyles would really hit Jerry. He would find himself left alone for a few moments in the living room of a beautiful home. *What a nice home,* he would think. *And what a nice room, and front yard with a stream running through it.* He had always wanted a place with a stream. There was a little dam and a waterwheel, and the landscaping was beautiful, not to mention the two-car garage and the workshop that Jerry dreamed of adding to year after year until he would have it altered to perfection. *Enough of this,* he decided. *I can't have it, so there's no use dreaming about it.* He moved away from the window and eased himself down on the beautifully upholstered sofa. Matthew 19:29 came to mind: "And everyone who has left houses or brothers or sisters or father or mother or children or farms for My name's sake, shall receive many times as much, and shall inherit eternal life."

Well, I don't have a house, Jerry reasoned. *But this house is as good as mine for the day. I don't hold the deed to it, but it's mine for as long as I'm here. And according to that verse, as long as I'm sacrificing for His name's sake, I've got many times as many homes all over the world wherever and whenever I need them!* There were homes of wonderful Christians all over the U.S. and the world who had opened their places to him and his wife. There was even the man on Biak island in Indonesia who had put him up.

A man could envy or resent the owner of such a home, and he could covet it. Or he could be thrilled with it and claim it as his own, as God's provision for his need. And from that day on, Jerry Reeder would do just that. There would be many more lessons to learn, including learning to claim the same blessing and promise when having to give up one's children to boarding schools, but a big one was out of the way.

The matter of pride had already been dealt with by that time. In fact the pride that a self-determined young pilot brings with him to the mission field, the kind that looks to his own wits and moxie to get him through, had been reckoned with during Jerry's first six months in Irian.

Jerry didn't do much flying at first. Mechanical problems grounded some of the planes, and the national fuel shortage delayed the delivery of needed replacement parts—particularly cylinders. And when planes and fuel *were* available, they had to be conserved for crucial flights. MAF provides the only air service to the interior, and much of its good relationship with the government depends on its willingness to fly supplies and people to the interior when necessary. In conserving planes and fuel for such trips and for the essential flights to serve area missionaries, MAF had trouble arranging enough flight time for Jerry's final field checkout and practice landings at the dozens of tiny airstrips hacked out of the acres upon acres of mountain foliage. Many of the strips had before-noon curfews, due to the tricky valley crosswinds.

But within a few months, Jerry began making solo flights and delivering food and supplies to missionaries. At 10:00 A.M. December 10, 1966, his Cessna 185 was loaded to gross capacity as he made his final approach to the earthen "runway" at the Regions Beyond Missionary Union station at Karubaga, situated at the end of a boxed-in canyon with mountains on both sides and at the far end. (Level sites for airstrips are virtually nonexistent. The strips are built uphill so the pilots can use the incline to slow the plane upon landing, and use the decline to generate speed for taking off.)

Jerry was in the landing configuration, flaps down, airspeed slowed to about sixty miles per hour, when he realized that he had not yet reeled in the fifty-foot antenna wire that trailed the plane. It was a minor matter, really. The wire is unwound after takeoff and manually reeled back in before final approach. If it's not reeled in, it could snap off upon landing and would cost the pilot about five dollars worth of wire. That's all.

Jerry knew he didn't have time to reel in the wire before landing, and though he doesn't remember consciously making the decision to pull out and swing around for another approach—giving him time to save the wire—suddenly the throttle was in full. The die had been cast.

The Cessna struggled over the airstrip, but it wouldn't climb. The uphill slope at the far end seemed to rush at Jerry. He decided to just try to hold her level for the length of the strip, then accelerate to make the turnaround and head back out of the three-sided box. He couldn't pull the flaps up because he would immediately lose altitude. There just wasn't any of that to spare, with the airstrip sloping up to the mountain at the far end. He was flying too fast and was too far down the strip to even consider landing, yet he was going too slow and was flying too low to be sure of pulling off the turnaround. But he had to try it. A weak and risky turnaround carried better odds than a head-on collision with a mountain. But only slightly.

Halfway into the maneuver Jerry's lack of airspeed cost him the lift necessary to stay airborne. The engine stalled. The plane wasn't spinning or nose-diving, but in pilot talk, it was "mushing down." Jerry was helpless, no longer in command of the power that made him the aircraft's master rather than its vulnerable victim. The talent he thought would bring him through as a wilderness pilot was worth nothing now. He was a passenger in an unguided missile and all he could do was keep it from pitching straight down and pray that it wouldn't burst into flames upon impact.

His downward speed increased. The rocky ridge filled the windshield; then Jerry saw only trees, branches, leaves, ferns. Screaming, "Oh no!" he added his life's most sincere prayer, "Help me!" He believed he would be killed, but his brain would not let him consciously experience the impact. He passed out before the plane smashed into the ridge. The cargo pod, the ailerons, the wheels, and the propeller were ripped from the fuselage and left at the top of the ridge when the plane careened back down the cliff, cartwheeling to a ledge nearly two hundred feet below, blowing the doors open, folding one wing under, buckling the floor into a clump of crunched aluminum. The 900 pounds of cargo in a net behind Jerry had miraculously remained intact. Still unconscious—he would never remember leaving the plane—Jerry unfastened his safety belts and crawled out past the wing tip. He awoke a few seconds later on his back, totally confused, without memory of where he was or what had happened. The hot morning sun shone in his eyes.

A small band of Dani tribesmen scrambled to his side and babbled in their own dialect, which he couldn't understand. In his limited Indonesian he tried to ask questions, but they couldn't understand and he could hardly talk for the pain and obstruction in his throat. He craned his neck to get a look at what was left of his plane, and the enormity of it hit him. Remembering stories of pilots who survive such wrecks only to live paralyzed for the rest of their days, Jerry carefully tested each appendage. He wiggled toes and fingers, bent knees and elbows, rolled shoulders and hips and ankles. Pain shot through his back, all the way down the spine. His ankles were tender and sore and he wondered if he had shattered bones in them the way his buddy Dave Hoisington had when he crashed eighteen months before.

The cartilage in his throat was mutilated, so it was just as well that Jerry couldn't swallow. It would have killed him. He tasted blood in his throat and it gagged him, but the swallow reflex

mechanism had been traumatized. He was getting just enough
air to stay alive and he didn't dare take a deep breath for fear
he'd strangle on the blood. Nevertheless, he was strangely
calm.

"So, this is what it's come to, Lord," he prayed silently.
"There's nothing I can do. Even with these blue skies and
bright sun and cool breezes, I'm helpless. I'm in your hands; it's
all in your hands now, Lord." He knew one of two things would
happen in the next instant. He would either start to recover, or
he would start to die. He waited to see which it would be, for it
really didn't matter. He had been brought to a point of
complete—though as he now says, involuntary—surrender.

Ironically, the first pilot to see the wreckage from the air was
Bob Johanson, whose slide show had been instrumental in
leading the Reeders to Irian Jaya. The Regions Beyond Missionary Union (RBMU) station had already radioed MAF at Sentani
that they had lost sight of the scheduled plane. A quick check of
the assignment board told Sentani that it was Jerry in the
Cessna. Work stopped. Personnel gathered around the radio. A
few moments later, Johanson's voice rasped through the static.
"Wreckage is below me. Plane is a total loss. I don't think he
made it." Lips tightened. Eyes darted and filled. Nothing was
said. The whole of the MAF compound at Sentani felt the
tension. The word spread quickly from the radio room to the
rest of the base that Jerry Reeder had been killed. George
Boggs went to Ethel Reeder's door with the awful news. He
stood there in tears and she knew. For forty-five minutes she
lived with the knowledge that her young husband was gone
after six months on the field, thousands and thousands and
thousands of miles from home.

Within fifteen minutes of the crash, nurses from the RBMU
station had administered a painkiller, and Jerry was carried
back up the ridge to the mission station. Half conscious, he was
terrified of the ride on the stretcher, certain he would be
thrown off and would plunge down the cliff again.

Johanson had determined to land and get the details so he

could give a full report to everyone listening to the radio. He would be documenting the death of the new pilot. But once at the station, when it became apparent that the throat cartilage damage, the sprained ankles, and the spinal injury were the extent of Jerry's injuries, Bob raced for the radio with the good news.

A doctor and nurse monitored Jerry all night. At one point the doctor wanted him to cough to clear his throat. "I can't," Jerry said. "I'm afraid I'll strangle."

"I've got a knife in that little black bag over there that can cut a clean hole through your throat to bypass the area with a tracheotomy, if you prefer," the doctor said. Jerry coughed.

Ethel joined him the next day and flew with him to Port Moresby in Papua New Guinea (about 800 air miles away), where he was fed through tubes in his nose for eight days before being shipped back for two months of convalescing in Sentani.

The excruciating spinal pain lasted six months, but during the last four of those, Jerry Reeder flew again anyway. He was terrified when Bob Johanson first took him out for easy landings in calm weather and put him through the paces. Even when Bob was handling the landings, Jerry found himself reliving the pre-impact horror of his crash. When Bob angled toward a mountain to prepare for landing, Jerry fought the tension.

A rule of thumb in jungle flying is that a pilot visually spots a potential landing area, a clearing, a sand bar, anything that might support an emergency put down, keeps his eye on it, mentally plots what approach he might use should his engine fail, and keeps the area in sight until he's out of its range. Jerry had always done this religiously, but now it drove him crazy. Each time he tried to plot how he would put the plane down if necessary, he flashed to his aborted pull out attempt. He didn't know how long he could take it. For awhile he even took to reading a magazine while cruising, peeking out over the top of it every few seconds to keep the plane steady and level and the instruments monitored.

It was nearly a year before Jerry felt totally confident piloting solo again, and even then, his pride had almost dissolved. If he found a rough spot where the winds seemed to make a landing impossible, rather than announcing that he wasn't going to try it and that no one else should either—as he might have done formerly—he was enough at peace with himself to be able to ask another pilot to try it. It was no longer, "If I can't do it, no one can." Now it was, "If I can't do it, perhaps someone else could." He was beginning to know himself.

JERRY REEDER
November 1969

But Jerry's victory over pride had a counterbalance of defeats too. Here he was, a sacrificing missionary pilot, looked up to, even idolized, yet he was beginning to feel spiritually dead. His walk was inconsistent. He battled impure thoughts. His prayer life suffered as he endured a roller coaster spiritual journey. Life and death adventure on the mission field became routine, and Jerry began looking forward to 1969 as he had never looked forward to a year before. It would mean the end of his and Ethel's first three years and eight months in Irian, and they would return to the States in December for their first furlough.

The discovery of the root of his spiritual problem upon his return home would change his life, but it was November of 1969, the month before the one he so longed for, that held the most bizarre experience of his young life to date.

Jerry Reeder was beginning to mellow. There had been times during his first term that his idealism and temper had gotten him into trouble. He had even shot off his mouth a few times too many. And there was reason not to do that.

Rebel forces were threatening a coup in Irian Jaya. Nationalist forces had to be transported all over the islands, and much of the taxi work fell to Mission Aviation Fellowship. The pilots had to keep to themselves their ideas about the revolution. It was not their place to take sides.

MAF personnel had to walk a precarious line. Their personal and spiritual ideals might dictate that they oppose plundering and occasional acts by individual soldiers that appeared without reason or cause—the type of thing seen in any war. Yet this was not their fight, not their calling.

Pilots like Jerry knew that the nationalist defense against revolutionary forces was largely dependent upon MAF personnel and equipment. And in moments of brashness, he said what he thought, representing only himself. If he saw a soldier with clothing or equipment he recognized, he'd say, "That came straight from ———'s store, didn't it?" And once he refused to fly some soldiers and their chickens out to the coast. He knew that even their own government forbade them from intimidating tribespeople into selling them chickens for pennies, which they in turn sold for dollars.

Many of Jerry's Indonesian friends told him they worried that he would get himself shot. "I was brash, naive, dumb," he admits now. "I would probably be able to quell my emotions today. But not then."

Once during the height of the insurgence, Jerry was assigned to pick up a mission carpenter named Dinus, a national who had been working at a station called Ilaga. Jerry fought his way through the fog and rain that nearly choked off the long narrow valley leading to the airstrip and landed against a strong wind. That meant he would have to take off with a tailwind, tricky and dangerous.

The Cessna had hardly stopped when Jerry leaped from the plane. "We don't have much time, Dinus," he said. "I can't take a whole lot of weight with this downwind situation and I don't have time to help you load much."

Dinus pointed to a pile of equipment and two mature pigs. "I have to take the pigs," he pleaded. "They are for my family's Christmas feast!"

"I'm sorry, I just can't spare the weight." Jerry had flown pigs before. He would have had to tie their legs to a pole and wrap burlap bags around them for diapers. Even then they would squeal and squeak, and they had been known to kick open a door. "I can't do it, Dinus."

"OK, take the pigs and leave me. I'll walk."

Jerry was losing patience—and time. "I'm not going to do that. You can't expect me to risk my life in this weather to carry pigs around. You get in with a few of your bags and I promise that the next time I get in here with an empty plane, I'll pick up the pigs for you."

As Dinus began to gather his cargo, Jerry noticed the ever-present military man who seemed to be on hand at every landing strip those days during the uprising. He was leaning way into the plane and looking all around. Jerry knew that when military men looked into airplanes, things tended to disappear. He walked up behind the officer, grabbed him by his uniform jacket, yanked him out of the way, and brushed right past him to his business of making room for Dinus's load. When Jerry turned around to see if Dinus was coming, he got his first look at the soldier, standing there stiff as a ramrod and sputtering, humiliated before the crowd of tribespeople who surrounded the scene.

Jerry realized immediately what he had done. He had blown it and there was no way around it. "Please forgive me," he said earnestly. "I'm in a hurry and under a lot of pressure, and I'm worried about this weather. I'm sorry. I shouldn't have grabbed you like that."

The officer stared at him coldly. His hands cradled a rifle, but he never raised it. Jerry turned to the crowd and explained in dialect: "I offended this man and I apologize to all of you. I was wrong, and it was a bad thing to do."

The officer spoke. "I am human too," he said. "I am human too." He would not reconcile, so Jerry told Dinus to jump in the plane. As Jerry climbed in he noticed two catsup bottles tied together with rattan that the commandant at Nabire (NAH-bee-ray) had asked him to present to each patrol officer. Thinking it might help make amends, he grabbed the bottles and tossed them to the officer. "These are yours," he said. But the man made no attempt to catch them and the bottles smashed together upon impact with his chest, leaving his shirt gobbed with the red stuff.

Jerry tried to apologize again to him and to everyone, but the man would not accept it, so Jerry and Dinus took off quickly.

The officer was not there the next time Jerry landed, so he left a new shirt for him. The next time Jerry landed, the man greeted him with a big smile and insisted upon having his picture taken with Jerry. It could have been much, much worse.

This was not the only just-before-furlough adventure. For a year and a half, Jerry had been asking around to see if any other pilots knew anything about the wreckage of an old plane he had seen in the highlands once. No one else had ever noticed it. Jerry was intrigued and determined to take a closer look. He had first seen it when flying from Sentani to a coastal station at Kokono in a turbo-supercharged plane that flew higher than the average Cessna. He had decided to fly straight through at a high altitude and enjoy a sightseeing tour of the snow-capped interior peaks. While crossing the ranges he was distracted by something shiny. There were no streams or puddles in the area so he backtracked a bit to see what it was. He caught sight of the wreckage of a plane, but it was isolated in a tiny canyon gorge and he couldn't get a good enough or long enough look at it to even determine what type of plane it was. Determining to come back on his own time someday to check it out, he was disappointed a couple of weeks later when his memory of the landmarks failed him and he was unable to locate it. Several weeks later he again failed to find it, but now he was hooked. He knew he'd find it, and he wanted to know what it was all about.

Now, a year and a half later, he found himself flying over the same range with a full fuel supply and an empty plane. He looked at his watch and made a note of the time. *As of right this minute,* he told himself, *I'm chartering this plane. I'm going to look for that wreckage and pay for the fuel myself.*

After ten minutes of circling, he found the wreckage again. Once more he was frustrated by not being able to get the right angle on it to tell anything specific. He flew back to his temporary base at Nabire and told his friend Mike Cremer of the DeLong Lumber Company (a survey crew from America), what he had seen.

Mike was the superintendent of the crew and had access to the company's turbine-powered Bell Jet Ranger helicopter. He found himself just as curious as Jerry was and suggested they have a look in the helicopter. "If you've got the money, we've got the time," he said.

Jerry was hardly wealthy, but he had to know what secrets this mountain wreckage held. They planned their assault, and as soon as he could, Jerry paid for the time and fuel on the MAF plane and flew in two drums of jet fuel for the helicopter. The Ranger pilot, Harold Wysong, took Jerry and Mike interior and pushed the limits of the 'copter's altitude capabilities by chugging near the wreckage at 13,500 feet. It was the day before Thanksgiving, 1969.

They chose a small flat rock near the site for a helipad, and Harold announced that he would try to hover near it. "If I can hover, I can land and take off again. But if I can't hover, that means I can't take off again once I land." The pilot's caution paid off when he discovered that he could not hover. He pulled away and descended to about 11,000 feet to see if he could hover there any better. He couldn't. He went down to about 10,000 feet and found a plateau at the end of a huge sink hole about 500 feet across and 500 feet deep. On the lip of the sink hole was a flat rock, and Harold discovered that he could hover near it, so he put the craft down.

"I think I can take off and land at 13,500 feet if I take just one of you at a time," Harold shouted over the din of the rotors. Jerry had discovered the wreckage first, and Mike was a gentleman, so he let Jerry go first. Mike stepped out and Harold took Jerry back up, but in the rarified atmosphere of the higher altitude it was obvious that Harold would still not be able to take off if he landed. He dropped back down to the 11,000 foot mark and landed. Jerry was eager to jump out and climb to the wreckage.

Harold shouted to him, "I'll give you forty-five minutes to run up there and check it out and I'll meet you back here! I don't have time to bring Mike back up with this weather closing in, and I don't want to shut the engine off at this altitude and run the risk of not being able to start it again. I'll wait down there with Mike. See you in forty-five minutes!"

Harold pulled the craft out of sight, and Jerry was alone. He stood on the side of a mountain at 11,000 feet with a machete in one hand and a radio in the other. Surveying the area quickly, he realized that the easiest way to go up would be first to go down and over. Rather than climb over each canyon and crevice, he would go to the bottom of the main canyon and then straight up about a thirty degree incline to the wreckage 2,500 feet above.

He started down the crevice toward the uphill side and found himself on a narrow ledge with his back pressed against the rock. *Wait a minute*, he thought. *If I so much as slip or turn my ankle—* He edged back to where the 'copter had landed and started downhill for a safer route. He wound up on the canyon floor where the terrain was spongy moss and mud. It wasn't hard climbing from there, and Jerry thought he had memorized the way from the air. But as he looked across at the side canyons, he didn't recognize anything. He walked and walked until he became convinced that he had gone too far. He went back down, looking in each canyon for the wreckage, but a cloud bank rolled up over the mountain, just as Harold had predicted, and clamped down over the area. *I've had it now*, Jerry decided. *If I don't get back to the rendezvous point, I could be stranded here overnight.*

Jerry ran down, hoping to find his way back. Then he heard the helicopter overhead. He could just see its shadow in the fog. "Harold, you're right over me," he radioed.

"Then go straight south to a clear valley," came the reply. "I'll go over there and wait for you."

Jerry scrambled down and over a ridge, puffing and chugging through the mountains for about twenty minutes. When he broke into the clear out from under the cloud, sure enough, there were Harold and the chopper, circling. There was no place to land. It was all boulders. Jerry radioed the bad news to Harold. "What about that rock in front of you?" Harold countered.

Though quite large, it reminded Jerry of a doghouse—sloped on either side. Jerry was dubious. "Wait right there," Harold insisted.

He brought the craft in carefully and gently rested the skids on the edge of the rock, calling Jerry one more time on the radio. "Climb aboard real slow so I can maintain balance." Jerry was excited but not scared. He for sure didn't want to spend a frigid night in these mountains. He pulled himself into the cockpit and felt the cold aluminum on his cheek. He stole a peek at the altimeter. It read 13,000 feet, much too high for the helicopter to hover or take off. Harold half slid, half flew the 'copter away from the rock and followed the slope downward, trading altitude for airspeed. The craft leaned and pitched but Harold brought her around and headed back down to the ridge at 10,000 feet to pick up Mike.

Rain surrounded the mountain and the valley, but Harold kept the Ranger in a thin dry hole and made his way down. He landed at the edge of the sink hole, and a freezing Mike, having just withstood a sleet storm in his shirt sleeves, shiveringly crawled in. Harold pulled the throttle and took off directly over the deep sink hole. Jerry heard popping noises from the engine. He didn't know what was happening but he knew it wasn't good. The altitude had been too much for the engine and increasing the throttle would stall her out. "Here we go," Harold said ominously as he throttled back and the craft descended slowly into the sink hole. *So this is the way it's going to end,* Jerry thought. *We'll hit hard at the bottom and if we're not maimed too badly, it'll take us two weeks to walk out of here.* He was convinced he had come to the end of his life.

Harold struggled to maintain some semblance of flight altitude so he could put the craft down flat at the bottom rather than spinning or tumbling. There would be no taking off from the bottom of the sink hole, of course. Mike leaned forward from the back seat. "I walked around the rim of this thing," he shouted. "There's a big crack in the side of it. Keep looking to your left!"

Still descending rapidly, Hal maneuvered to the left and immediately saw the big chunk cut from the side of the sink hole like a crack in a giant coffee cup. He directed the struggling Ranger out through the crack and descended safely to 9,000 feet where reducing power and cooling the engine brought it to life again. He chugged back toward the base in the rain, now the least of their problems. Flying in the soup is harrowing, but it seemed nothing compared to what they had just endured.

While he was glad to be alive, Jerry figured he had blown his big chance to check out the wreckage. Then Mike leaned forward. "What are you doing tomorrow?" he said.

"It's Thanksgiving," Jerry said. "I won't be making any runs."

"Want to try it again?" Mike asked.

Jerry smiled.

JERRY REEDER
Thanksgiving Day, 1969

Jerry could hardly sleep that night at Nabire.

He and Mike Cremer had assembled survival kits and backpacks, items that would have given them at least a little more peace of mind and less of a sense of urgency had they had them during the first attempt.

Harold Wysong had studied the manual on the jet helicopter and noted that in an emergency at high altitude he could push the engine a certain percentage past the temperature red line for a few seconds. Equipped with that emergency power performance—and rationalizing that this once-in-a-lifetime peek into a never-before uncovered plane crash was indeed an emergency—he decided he could put Mike and Jerry down at 13,500 feet and be certain to take off again.

After more than a year and a half of enduring the wary looks of people who thought he'd been seeing things, Jerry was going to get a good look at the old wreckage. To his knowledge, no one else on earth had ever seen it. He would bring back photos and physical evidence to prove his sanity.

The next morning the weather was good, and Harold's calculations were correct. He put down about fifteen minutes' walking distance from the crash site, and Mike and Jerry piled out with their gear. Harold said he'd see them in two hours.

When the helicopter was out of earshot, the only sound was the hurried crunch of the two men's feet as they scrambled over the rocks. Finally they came up over a small ridge and the tail section of a DC-3 came into view. Their pace slowed as they carefully took stock of the entire scene. They were speechless.

Before touching anything or even thinking of moving any part of the wreckage, they counted fourteen skeletons. More were buried in the debris. Jerry recognized the craft as Australian and found a magazine dated 1945 containing stories about the atomic bomb and about servicemen returning home to look for jobs. Jerry removed dog tags from three of the skeletons.

The cabin section had been burned out, but the bodies of the pilot and co-pilot lay in the cockpit. Their chart case had been burned around the edges, but the charts were still readable. Perhaps they would show where the plane was headed, what caused the crash, and when it went down. The relatives of these victims had lived twenty-four years knowing only that their loved ones were last seen taking off. They had likely long since given up hope of seeing them alive again, but to a person, they must have entertained nagging questions and wondered if they would ever even get confirmation of their losses.

Mike and Jerry decided that the skeleton with the smaller head and still wearing high-heeled military shoes had to be that of a nurse. The stretchers strewn around showed that the plane had been carrying wounded.

Not far away Jerry found the cargo doors lodged across the top of a small ravine, sheltering a life raft covered with a rotted blanket. Someone had survived the crash and had built this makeshift temporary home. Jerry and Mike shot rolls and rolls of film. They worked quickly and silently, saying little more than, "Over here," and, "Look at this."

Jerry climbed a cliff behind the wreckage to get a photograph of the entire site from a better angle, but he found himself winded so quickly that he had to stop and sit on a rock. He realized that it would have been nearly impossible for anyone to have walked away from the scene at such an altitude. As his breathing became less labored he realized that he had been scurrying around the wreckage and had not sat still since they landed. Mike worked quietly below him, picking through the debris. Jerry heard only a breeze, a few swallows darting about the area, and a gentle, steady, rhythmic squeaking noise.

He squinted and looked for the source of the sound. The rudder of the plane moved slowly, very slightly, back and forth in the wind. The noise had been generated for more than two decades, but no one had heard it until now.

Mike and Jerry gathered a few things, including Dutch New Guinea coins and other trinkets, and headed back to the helipad. Returning from their flight, they turned over their physical evidence to the Australian embassy in Singapore. Such a stir hadn't been seen there for years. The Aussies faced a mountain of red tape trying to convince the Indonesian government to let them come in and investigate the wreckage. Eventually permission was granted, and they flew in with a huge fleet of aircraft, including two Hercules, each of which carried a helicopter and a radio and weather-monitoring craft.

Jerry rode in the lead plane with a team of eleven and spotted the site for them. Then he was flown out and the research team stayed, intending to spend a week combing the area. As it turned out, they were able to spend only two hours, just as Mike and Jerry had, because of the lack of oxygen at that altitude. They gathered all the bones they could and returned them for burial. The pilot's case Jerry had uncovered showed that the chart for the area had indicated that the highest terrain in the locale was 11,000 feet above sea level. The plane had flown at about 13,000 feet—probably for safety—but in reality the highest peak was closer to 16,500 feet.

The news of the discovery hit the Australian papers and one woman wrote to Jerry. Her husband had been a male nurse and was returning on the plane to see the son who had been born while he was at war. His letters had talked of his looking forward to coming back to Australia to begin life again with his family. The woman thanked Jerry for helping close the final chapter on what had been a mystery in her life. She had believed for years that the craft had been lost at sea.

The nurse Mike and Jerry had identified happened to be the first Australian nurse killed in World War II. And her death had occurred, ironically, on the way home.

Having learned to expect the unexpected on the mission field, Jerry knew that flying a plane in the jungles of Irian Jaya would bring him experiences that few men would face in their lifetimes. But spotting that wreckage and realizing how easy it would have been to have missed it, or to have decided not even to fly across that range in the first place, made him realize that he had been privileged to encounter one bizarre personal incident that hardly anyone anywhere could match. He couldn't hope for another.

His next adventure was to be a spiritual one, and it was every bit as meaningful—in the long run, more so—than his mountain odyssey.

JERRY REEDER
Late 1969–early 1970

By the end of the Reeders' first three years and eight months in Irian Jaya, Jerry had long been aware that by and large he was living a defeated Christian life. That explained his encounters with the military and his fleshly reactions to numerous other confrontations. He was inconsistent in his attitude toward the things of God, and he was unable to maintain a regular Bible reading and prayer time. His prayers usually ended in a confused sentence or two. He battled fear, among other things; yet he had enough training and background to be painfully aware of the biblical injunction of Christ, "Be ye holy, for I am holy."

Jerry knew he could never and would never be perfect, but the ominous command from God brought a sense of hope as well as foreboding, because it intimated that there might be hope—if the Lord had said it—for him to at least start moving in the direction of a sanctified life to go along with his sanctified spiritual position in Christ. Jerry really wanted a consistent and deep walk with God, but he didn't make any progress in his personal and private rededications and resolutions—until he happened to hear a series of tapes.

They had been recorded by suburban Wichita, Kansas, pastor Ernest B. Rockstad in his seminar on exposing the

powers of darkness. In his "Setting the Captives Free,"
Rockstad spoke on the believer's resources in Christ through
union with Him, based on Romans 6. He emphasized the
reality of the activity of demons and introduced listeners to
spiritual warfare while hammering home the fact that the
Christian is equipped with the weapons for victory.

It was all new to Jerry. Could a Christian be oppressed by
demons? By the late 1970s it was common knowledge in the
United States that some conservative evangelical ministers
were engaged in overt combat with demons that oppressed and
in many cases seemed to possess professing Christians. But a
decade earlier, the subject polarized believers. It seemed
incredible and many would rather not even have thought about
it. True enough, such warfare is not for every Christian, but
Jerry was intrigued by the idea that he was not seeing any
progresss in his struggle to walk closer to the Lord because of
the possibility of a concerted plan by the powers of darkness to
impede his spiritual growth. To him it seemed more than just
his living in the flesh in a sinful world of temptation; maybe
there was something else, and maybe this Rockstad had some
advice Jerry could heed that would lead the way to victory. He
had never been involved in the occult or Satan worship, but
perhaps he was a target of such power because of the strategic
ministry to which the Lord had called him.

Rockstad's messages encouraged addressing the spirits directly. At first Jerry was afraid to. He thought about it for weeks
and weeks, but still could not bring himself to try it. When he
had the courage, he didn't feel particularly oppressed, and
when he *did* feel burdened, he didn't have the courage. He was
fascinated by the possibility, but he wasn't yet totally convinced
of the validity of the whole thing. It was out of his realm of
experience, and there was comfort in staying in a familiar niche.

Then came the night he was working on a flight schedule
alone in his office. It was about ten o'clock and his mind was
wandering. He set aside his work and decided, *I think I'll try it*

now. Opening his Bible to Romans 6, he reminded himself of the believer's union with Christ by reading the fifth through the fourteenth verses:

> For if we have become united with Him in the likeness of His death, certainly we shall be also in the likeness of His resurrection, knowing this, that our old self was crucified with Him, that our body of sin might be done away with, that we should no longer be slaves to sin; for he who has died is free from sin.
>
> Now if we have died with Christ, we believe that we shall also live with Him, knowing that Christ having been raised from the dead, is never to die again; death no longer is master over Him. For the death that He died, He died to sin, once for all; but the life that He lives, He lives to God. Even so, consider yourselves to be dead to sin, but alive to God in Christ Jesus.
>
> Therefore do not let sin reign in your mortal body that you should obey its lusts, and do not go on presenting the members of your body to sin as instruments of unrighteousness; but present yourselves to God as those alive from the dead, and your members as instruments of righteousness to God. For sin shall not be master over you, for you are not under law, but under grace (NASB).

That's terrific, Jerry thought. *That's just what I want. According to this Scripture, it's already been accomplished. Why can't I have it? Why can't I make it work?* He knelt to pray: "Lord, I reaffirm my faith in You. I consider myself dead to sin but alive to You in Christ Jesus." He then turned his attention to the powers of darkness. "If there are any unclean spirits or evil demons or whatever you call yourselves here who are responsible in any way for impeding my spiritual growth, then I see you in direct opposition to the command of the Lord Jesus Christ who said, 'Be ye holy, for I am holy.'

"Because of that, I do what it says in Ephesians 6:10 and 11: 'Finally, be strong in the Lord, and in the strength of his might . . . that you may be firm against the schemes of the devil.' I bring the might of the Lord Jesus Christ against you who are standing in opposition to His command for my life, and I resist you and command you out of my life. In the name of Jesus Christ, leave me and go wherever He is sending you."

Nothing happened. Jerry had done everything Rev. Rockstad had advised in the tapes. He had quoted appropriate Scripture, he had addressed the demons directly, he had rebuked them, commanded them to leave, and claimed the victory. Rockstad had also said that it might be necessary to repeat the commands several times. Jerry repeated his prayer and his rebukes a half dozen times. Suddenly, with no warning, his body began to tremble. It was as if he were scared to death, standing atop a high, quivering scaffold; yet he felt no fear, only the shaking. "I was a disinterested observer, watching myself tremble." As he repeated the commands once more, the sensation of fear began to engulf him.

"I became aware of loathsome, unclean, foul personalities. I didn't panic, but I was in dread fear. As my fear escalated, however, I was aware of the presence of the Holy Spirit indwelling me and comforting me with reminders that He was there to protect me. He brought to mind many verses to assure me that Jesus Christ dwells in me and God dwells in Him, so God the Father was there with me."

Jerry resisted the temptation to panic, and after a minute, the trembling stopped as quickly as it had begun. He felt complete release from the powers of darkness. For more than fifteen minutes he poured out his praise and petitions to God, feeling a real communion with Him for the first time in months. "It was not really dramatic," Jerry remembers. "It was just a sweet time of reunion with my Lord."

It would be a couple of years before Ethel completely understood what Jerry tried to tell her about that night. He thought she too could experience the same kind of freedom, but as Jerry would find, it was only the beginning for him. He would discover that he had scored a general victory over the dark powers of Satan, but it wouldn't keep him from being a phony. It wouldn't be a cure-all experience to set him up as a spiritual giant. And when he returned to the United States for several months on furlough and people put him on the missionary's pedestal and expected him to say what they wanted to hear about life on the field, that experience did not keep him from faking it, from being shallow. He had simply challenged the powers in his life in a general way, and until he dealt with some specifics, and until he appropriated the victory on an intelligent, regular basis and established a consistent walk, he would remain disappointed and defeated.

He was quickly back in the old rut. He faked his way through deputation. His prayer life was shot. He could pray eloquently in public, and he continued to satisfy people's expectations by talking about the glory and blessing of a life committed to serving Christ in the remotest jungles of the world. But on the way back to his room each night he found himself dejected, introspective, flat. There was no life, no victory. He knew he was being oppressed again, but he didn't like the idea of having to confront evil spirits every time he wanted victory. He didn't want to face a life of emotional and fearful confrontation. The Scriptures said he was crucified with Christ, so why couldn't he live like it? Why couldn't he get the upper hand over all the temptation and inconsistency? All he could pray at the end of each day before falling into bed was, "Lord, help me." He figured he would just have to wait for more light on the subject and until then he would put the whole thing on a back shelf somewhere and try to forget about it.

But he couldn't. After a message he gave in a church in Buffalo, New York, in early 1970, Jerry was invited to eat at the home of one of the members, Arlan Witlinger, a plumber. It wasn't long before Jerry realized that this man had the kind of victorious Christian life that he himself longed for. Arlan seemed to be living a true New Testament life, the kind Jerry knew would bring happiness and contentment. He determined that as soon as the meal was over, he would treat this new friend as a counselor and tell him the truth. Jerry would open up to him and see if Arlan couldn't untangle the confusion and help lead him to real peace with God.

Jerry found it hard to concentrate on cordial table conversation. He was thinking about how to broach the subject of his real concern with Arlan. His opening came later when they were alone. Jerry jumped right into it. "What would you say to someone that Romans 6 doesn't work for?"

"It doesn't work for you?"

"That's right. I keep coming back to it. I read a lot of books about people like Dawson Trotman and Hudson Taylor, and they all seem to refer to the spiritual secret of dying to self, based on Romans 6. I know the key must lie there, but it doesn't seem to work for me."

"How do you mean, it 'doesn't work'?" Mr. Witlinger asked.

"Well, I understand it, I believe it, and I have applied it, but I haven't realized the benefits of it. When temptation comes, I claim the promise in Romans 6 that I have been crucified with Christ, and I expect the temptation to leave. But it doesn't.

"The part of me that gives in to temptation is supposed to be dead and my spiritual being is to be alive to God through Christ Jesus. But the temptation, the impure thought, whatever, escalates. That proves that I'm not crucified in my fleshly, sin-prone body. I guess I really don't understand after all. According to that Scripture, reckoning myself dead to sin should release me. I see no other provision in God's Word to free me from my old nature except that identification of union with Christ.

"I hate to admit it, Arlan, but it has forced me to put all this on a back shelf and try to forget about it until I get some more light on the subject."

Jerry hoped he had not said too much, had not alienated this fine Christian man. He hoped Arlan was mature enough to realize that missionaries and missionary pilots were not unusual saints who had no problems. He hoped Arlan didn't have any preconceived notions about the spiritual status of the "full-time servant." As it turned out, Jerry needn't have worried.

"I'm not surprised things are working out for you the way they are," Arlan said.

"You're not? Why?"

"Don't you see what you're doing? You're standing on your experience and letting it be your foundation, your platform, your basis of operation. You're taking God's Word, which says you've been crucified with Christ, and you're examining it with your internal experience. When it doesn't line up with your experience, you assume that the Word of God must be wrong."

"I never thought of it that way, but I suppose you're right."

"Well, you've got it backwards," Arlan continued. "Do it this way: stand on God's Word, let God be your foundation, your platform, your basis of operation. Now take your *experience* and look at *it* from every angle. If that doesn't line up with God's Word, then reject your experience. You've been letting your experience tell you whether or not the Bible is valid when you should be letting the Bible tell you whether your experience is valid. When they don't agree, you should be rejecting your experience, not the Word of God."

"Oh, no, Arlan, you can't do that. You've gone too far too fast. I can't reject my own experience. Why, that's everything I am, all the decisions I've ever made, all my victories, all my defeats, my sum total. I can't reject that."

"Really," Arlan said patiently. "How's it working out?" Jerry raised his eyebrows and pursed his lips. Arlan paused, then continued: "Let me suggest something to you. You know we have a very powerful and clever enemy who is able to counterfeit just about anything. He even counterfeits many of the wonders of God. Do you suppose he could also counterfeit your old nature?"

"I'm listening," Jerry said.

"Do you suppose that just as often as you walk by faith to the cross and claim your crucifixion with Christ and gladly reckon yourself dead to sin—which, as you know and have said, is the basis on which you claim your freedom from your old nature—that Satan slips in a counterfeit old nature? Your sin nature is dead, crucified with Christ! You know it, you've claimed it, God has said it. But into your mind, your being, your body, Satan projects counterfeit evil desires that you are misconstruing as still coming from your old nature. If you are a Christian, they can only be counterfeits of Satan, the liar.

"Sure, temptation will come your way, and, sure, some of it will indeed be a product of your old nature which you must reckon dead daily. But if you resist and claim victory based on the very Word of God, to then say that the escalating temptation is a result of your old nature is to call God a liar. Who's the real liar?"

Jerry sat quietly and shook his head slowly. "That's a new one on me," he said. "I never thought of it, but it sure makes sense."

A few days later Jerry was tempted by impure thoughts. He didn't want to dwell on them and have them break his fellowship with God, but in himself he knew he didn't have the will power to resist. He quickly reviewed his own attitude toward Romans 6 and claimed the victory over his sin nature, which he clearly believed had been reckoned crucified with Christ and should thus no longer respond to such temptation. But the temptation increased in intensity. He thought of Arlan's counsel.

If this is God's only provision to free me from the old nature, then I am free or God is a liar. I'm not ready to admit that, because my whole salvation is based on His integrity. Therefore, what I am experiencing right now cannot be coming from my old nature. Jerry spoke directly to the powers of darkness: "I know you're here and I know why. You're trying to make it appear that the principle of Romans 6 doesn't work. I recognize these feelings that my old nature is still alive to sin as a lie straight from hell and I command you in the name of Jesus Christ to leave me and go wherever He sends you."

The evil desire was gone. Jerry felt free, nine feet tall, a living example of the phenomenon in James 4:7: ". . . Resist the devil and he will flee from you." This was his first taste of real and specific victory over such temptation since he had become a Christian. He had experienced the power of the indwelling Christ, and while he knew he would be tempted again and again, he finally learned that his old nature was indeed dead to sin when he claimed the promises in Romans 6. The continuing temptations in those situations could be dealt with as lies of Satan.

"It just amazed me," Jerry says. "I was surprised by grace. I realized that this was phase two in resisting temptation; it was resisting the devil himself. Deal with the old nature first because he who is dead is free from sin, but when that seems not to work, recognize it as a lie of Satan."

JERRY REEDER
1970–1972

Jerry's discovery was so revolutionary and so freeing that he shared it with many missionary friends. One mission leader stopped him at a crucial point. "Let me get this straight, Jerry," he said. "Do I understand you correctly that you knew and believed and understood Romans 6 and that you applied it?"

"That's right," Jerry said.

"But it didn't work?"

"That's right. For years and years it didn't work. Or I thought it didn't work. I figured my old nature must not really be dead, even though I know now that that meant God was a liar."

"Well, friend," the mission leader said, "you've been real honest with me, and I'm going to be real honest with you. That's where I am right now. Romans 6 doesn't work for me." Jerry was happy to be able to share how he had found victory.

After two years of talking about it and sharing it with friends, missionaries, church groups, and anyone who would listen, Jerry finally talked his wife Ethel into trying it for herself. She suffered from returning symptoms of rheumatic fever, from which she had recovered years before. "Wait a minute," she would say, "I went through this already and the Lord healed me. I consider these symptoms counterfeits from the enemy and I reject them in the name of Christ." Within a half hour, they were gone.

Jerry shared his new insight at churches any time he spoke at more than one service. He gave his standard missionary presentation at the first meeting, then got deeper into battling the lies of Satan in the second. And it continued to work for him too, not as a fetish or a magic trick, but because he finally understood the true nature and the extent of his lies. The peace of mind and the victory over sin pushed Jerry into a more consistent prayer life and Bible study program. Tenacious sins were headed off at the pass. If they were products of his old nature, he claimed Romans 6 and reckoned himself dead to the sin. If the temptation increased, he called it a lie of the devil and commanded it to leave in the name of Jesus Christ. He was a new man.

By mid-1972 Jerry had become known among his peers as a sensitive, spiritual man who cared about people, his family, and his work. He was looked up to by new missionaries, and MAF Area Vice President Ken Simmelink felt he was ready for a new level of responsibility. Jerry was safety-conscious and technically accomplished in flying, mechanics, and radio, so he was named program manager in Kalimantan (Kah-lee-MAHN-tahn), or Borneo.

The next two years would be enlightening for him as he would discover that leadership was not what motivated him; in fact, he would be happy when the time came to move back into a nonmanagement role. Meanwhile, there were lessons to be learned.

The first and toughest forced him back to Matthew 19:29, the promise that all sacrifices made for the sake of the name of the Lord would be compensated many times over. But rather than claiming it for the sacrifice of a nice home or wealth, he had to appropriate it for leaving his oldest son, Claude, behind in Sentani for the last six weeks of his first grade school year while

Jerry and Ethel and the younger boy went off to begin work in Kalimantan.

Claude had never been to Kalimantan and could not even form a mental picture of this place with the strange name somewhere off in the blue miles away. Jerry realized later that Claude was so confused and troubled over their early departure that he really gave up hope of ever seeing his family again.

When the school year was finally over, Claude traveled to Jakarta with one missionary family and then on with another to Kalimantan, where the Reeders met him at the airport. "That's the biggest sacrifice missionaries are called to, in my opinion," Jerry says. "It's not so much being away from their children for awhile; it's more not knowing what they think about all of it." But Jerry sees no alternative.

Some say separating children from their missionary parents at tender ages is a violation of biblical injunctions, that it's a modern-day missionary trapping, that maybe mission agencies should provide tutors so the kids can stay with their parents. It doesn't seem fair, but other than boarding school, solutions aren't practical. Jerry feels that "in order to get the job done and to prepare your children for modern society, you have to send them to school. It's just part of the lifestyle that you chose when you decided to follow Christ.

"In Sentani the kids go to school near the mission base, but at most other stations the kids have to go off somewhere. When it's not possible to have the child at home and in school at the same time, you leave your children for the sake of the name of the Lord and trust Him to compensate you and your child for that separation."

When he had arrived in Kalimantan Jerry didn't know he would be proving to himself that he didn't like managerial work. It was a small operation: two other men and three planes and plenty of work to go around. Jerry and Ethel did everything from seeing that what the missionaries ordered from the coast was purchased and flown in to them, to bookkeeping, billing, flight permissions, clearing parts through customs, maintaining the airplanes, repairing the radios, keeping radio contact with all the missionaries in the area, establishing and maintaining rapport with them, and flying interior regularly to deliver supplies and messages and personnel and to pick up the same.

Jerry enjoyed talking with the missionaries and finding out how MAF could better meet their needs. He even tried to inspire them to more imaginative uses of the airplane services. "I wasn't smart enough to delegate the detail work so I could concentrate on the managing of the program as I was supposed to," he says. Consequently he quickly felt burdened by the load and by the fall of 1972, just a few months after he had arrived, he had already sensed that he might not be looking farther than one brief term as program manager.

Ken Simmelink could see that the assignment was already costing Jerry his enthusiasm and inspiration, and while he wasn't falling down on the job, for the sake of the pilot and the program his term as program manager in Kalimantan would probably end when his next furlough came due. Then Jerry would likely be reassigned to technical duty, flying and working in the radio shop in Sentani (which is where the children can go to school without being separated from their parents). But that was more than a year and a half away.

The Fliers

JEFF HERITAGE
June 25, 1976

At the Netherlands Reformed Church base in Langda, 150 miles interior from Sentani, young rookie missionary helicopter pilot Jeff Heritage was staying with Jan and Janny Louwerse when the earthquake hit. He was half thrown out of bed with the first shock and thought he heard the mountains crashing down around him. He looked out the window, expecting everything to come in and cover him as he lay half in and half out of bed, but the night was too black. The noise was deafening. As he tried to stand, the floor shifted. He prayed, "Oh God, be with us."

The house sat next to a north/south runway. Jeff was in the northwest corner of the house. Parallel to the runway and about 200 yards from the house is a sheer drop of about 2500 feet. On the south side of the runway, the dropoff extends around and farther up the valley, leaving the house on a plateau, not a comfortable place in the dark when it sounds as if you are being alienated from solid ground.

The door leading out of the house is on the south end. When Jeff ran down the east/west hallway behind Jan, the house shifted to the east so he ran back the other way. The house tilted that way. "Jan, do you have a flashlight?" he screamed.

"No!"

"Get one before you open the door!" Jeff thought the entire plateau had broken away from the edge of the house and that he and Jan would be running out into thin air. He bet his life on it.

But Jeff's conviction that the base house teetered on the brink of an earthquake-caused cliff turned out to be just one of those tricks the mind plays when it has lost its equilibrium. Jeff and Jan were soon outside and safe.

The local village was right on the cliff and the tribespeople— none of whom were Christians yet—moaned and cried hysterically, clinging like children to Jan and Janny. The tremors continued for several minutes, as at every other station near the epicenter. The ground shook under Jeff's feet and he imagined the damage the landslides were doing as they filled in the gorges on every side.

All he could do was wait for daylight to see in just what situation he would find himself. Langda, because of its unique teacup style location, gets light about a half-hour later than most everywhere else in Irian. Jeff would be on the radio as soon as he could to see what other stations had been affected. There was always the chance that as bad as things were where he was, it was even worse elsewhere.

JEFF HERITAGE
Fall 1972—Winter 1974

Jeff Heritage was twenty-four years old. The third of ten children to American parents in Hawaii, he had been raised in California and Washington, met his future wife, Charolyn, in high school in Tacoma, married her in 1968 while attending U.S. Army flight training school, and flew helicopters in Viet Nam in 1969–70. Upon his return he was assigned to Fort Lewis, Washington, near his home, only to find that his oldest brother, John, had found religion.

John had become a Christian through the ministry of a local Lutheran pastor, but Jeff was skeptical. In fact, he didn't want anything to do with it. He was the typical hard-living, hard-drinking, dope-doing, macho helicopter pilot. He was probably even an alcoholic, he acknowledges now, but back then, everybody he ran with was into the same things. All but his wife.

Charolyn, who had become a Christian as a child, did not adopt Jeff's lifestyle, though she maintained no real consistent Christian witness either. She didn't study her Bible or pray much, but she continued to attend church. Charolyn had become a nominal Christian and had no basis for hassling her young husband. Still, his lifestyle was not for her.

By the fall of '72, Jeff had been out of the army for six months, but he still lived the free and easy life of the young officer pilot. He got a job in a real estate office and was doing moderately well, but his marriage was in shambles. His wife had had it.

Jeff began to see himself for what he was, but still he tried to avoid discussions with his brother. While there was an obvious difference in John, Jeff was still wary. He debated whether or not to accept John's invitation to visit one weekend in November, but he finally decided to go. He could easily shut off the religious talk if it bothered him, and John had always been careful not to push too hard or argue with Jeff (though he seldom missed an opportunity to speak up for his new faith).

The first couple of days of the visit were uneventful, and Jeff was able to stay out of religious discussions with John. But again, his brother's life was making an impact. Even Jeff's wife noticed. Then John's boss, Ray Dun, and his wife visited for Sunday dinner.

Here was a man who loved to share his faith. And when he discovered a live one in Jeff Heritage, he unloaded with both barrels. He made no apologies. He argued for his faith and lovingly attempted to persuade Jeff to see his point. Ray was a wealthy farmer with an elementary school education, and the urbane, educated, sophisticated helicopter pilot/real-estate broker couldn't relate to him at all. In an almost sadistic way, Jeff enjoyed baiting the old-timer. He patronized Ray for hours, keeping him witnessing and arguing and reading Scripture to counter Jeff's wisecracks. Jeff hardly listened, embarrassing his brother and his wife by stifling smiles and laughter all afternoon and on into the early evening. To him the whole scene was hilarious, but soon it was time to head home.

"Son," Ray said, "would you mind if we prayed with you and your wife that you'll have a safe trip home this evening?"

"Not at all," Jeff said with a smile. "That would be fine." Ray insisted that everyone join hands in a circle, which was almost too much for Jeff. It left him without a hand to cover his smirk, but he forced himself to go along with the gag.

They bowed their heads, and Ray said, "Repeat after me

silently if you feel in your heart that this is right." With that, he went into a recitation of the Four Spiritual Laws, repeating the same sort of witness he had maintained all day. While Jeff had laughed at it for hours, he was able to control himself now. And he recalled that while trying to trip up Ray earlier he had by some convoluted logic convinced himself of the existence of God.

As Ray prayed the prayer of repentance, forgiveness, and acceptance of Christ, what had seemed baloney all day long to Jeff now hit him between the eyes. It seemed right, just as Ray had said. Jeff silently prayed along. What he had kept at bay with a wall of laughter now pierced his heart. In an instant, the rough, tough veteran was on his knees, sobbing and thanking God.

A minute before he had been a lost skeptic. Now he had professed faith in Jesus Christ and asked Him to come into his life. "It's been different ever since," Jeff says. "I knew I was saved. I felt saved. I knew Jesus was in my life, and, for the first time, I knew He was real."

It would be a while before he understood why many Christians don't smoke and why some won't have even an occasional social drink. But he accepted a longstanding invitation to church and soon began appropriating in his life the love of God that would make him a better husband and a better father to his two young sons. "People prayed for me and helped me, and I began to seek God through His Word."

Thirty days after Jeff's conversion, God sent Bob Lee into his life. He was a new man at the real estate office, and Jeff discovered quickly that he was a Christian. They began spending a lot of time together at lunch and on break and after work, talking about their experience with God. Though Jeff continued to stumble and fall frequently just like any new child in the faith, Bob was just what he needed. Bob had attended Moody Bible Institute but had failed flight camp. Now he was working in real estate to put bread on the table while continuing to seek a ministry opportunity.

Jeff, the commercially successful agent with the new house and car and the marriage that would have failed in a month had it not been for his coming to Christ, was to train the new man; Bob, the mature Christian, returned the training by discipling Jeff, advising him spiritually, encouraging him in his walk with Christ.

After discovering their mutual interest in aviation, it wasn't long before Bob told Jeff about the missionary pilot organizations such as Wycliffe's Jungle Aviation and Radio Service (JAARS) and Mission Aviation Fellowship. It was all new to Jeff. But since he was the type who always looked for a reason for everything—even beyond Bob's having been brought into his life for spiritual guidance—he assumed that God had sent Bob to expose him to the possible uses of his talents to serve Christ in missionary aviation.

It wasn't enough for Jeff that his life had changed and that Char had seen enough to make her willing to try to salvage the marriage. It wasn't enough that the nightly martini with the boys that more often than not turned into an all-night gab session had long since ceased. Jeff wanted to do something for God, and maybe this was it. In the late spring of 1973, Jeff typed two letters, one to MAF and the other to JAARS. (He would discover the JAARS letter in his desk three months later; somehow he had not gotten around to mailing it.)

His letter told MAF of his background in helicopters, of his new faith, of his limited experience with fixed-wing aircraft (after tiring of helicopter duty in the army), and of his interest in serving Christ through his abilities.

When he received what he thought was a sort of don't-call-us-we'll-call-you type of reply a month later, informing him that MAF didn't fly helicopters and didn't see any in their immediate future, and that he would also need fixed-wing experience, commercial license, and aircraft and power-plant mechanic license, Jeff figured that the Lord was closing that door for practical reasons. "I thought God was as practical as I was," he recalls. "It would have been impractical for me to uproot my family right then. I had not yet progressed to that level of faith. If someone had told me then what some steps of faith entail, I would have told them they were crazy, irresponsible. I don't know what I would have done if MAF had said, 'OK, come on and join us.'"

While Jeff was practical in not wanting to uproot his family for the mission field, he was not too practical to uproot them for a better job. His and Char's best friends from army flight school—Dave and Carolyn Troxell—wrote them at just the right time, when the real estate market was getting tight and commissions were hard to come by. Dave had a proposition for Jeff.

He was running his own crop dusting business in Bowling Green, Ohio, and wanted to know if Jeff wanted to come back there and join him in building up the business. By February of 1974, Jeff had thought about it long enough. A house had been lined up for him to see, and a helicopter was ordered for his use in the business. He phased himself out of the real estate business and by Sunday night, June 1, 1974, his bags were packed and his airline ticket was on the table. He would scout out the house, work out the details, and come back to move his family east to Bowling Green. Just before he left, Carolyn called. She could hardly talk.

"Dave was spraying a field in the helicopter this afternoon," she managed. "One of the spray booms broke off and flew up into the main rotor system."

"Oh, no," Jeff said. "How bad?"

"It knocked off the tail rotor and he spun in from about a hundred and fifty feet."

"Fire?"

"Yes."

"And Dave?"

"Killed."

Carolyn and Char had been close when they lived together while Jeff and Dave had been in flight training. Char and Jeff flew to Ohio together to be with her, and while they were there, friends and family asked Jeff if he would still come and try to get the business going again. It probably was foolhardy, Jeff realizes now, but with all the emotion and upheaval, there was hardly a choice. He moved the family.

While working on a local farm just to make some money, learn the area, and get to know the farmers and their techniques, Jeff became almost as intrigued with agriculture itself as with crop spraying. He and Char began to look into buying a ranch of their own in Cascade, Montana. Jeff also received an offer from a man who owned two crop spraying outfits. He wanted Jeff to manage one of the two, either in Tucson, Arizona, or Cascade.

The coincidence was enough for Jeff. "It must be the Lord's will," he decided. But then he received another letter from MAF. They wanted a new résumé to update their helicopter file, and while Jeff didn't have all the training usually required, they had needs in Indonesia and Mexico and possibly elsewhere. They might be getting into helicopters. Now all the coincidental dovetailing just puzzled the Heritages. They didn't know what they were supposed to do; for starters, Jeff responded to MAF's letter with the requested information.

Meanwhile he and Char had found solid fellowship and were studying the Bible and growing like never before. Jeff even asked prayer from the men's group he was involved in. There was a sense that the Lord had something special in store for them soon, but the waiting was frustrating. Finally, he and Char put it to the Lord. "Just show us what You want us to do," they prayed.

Another couple of months went by with Jeff just working for a farmer, driving a tractor, and doing other heavy work. The weather was turning bitterly cold, and in a strange way he loved the battle with the elements. He was making good money and enjoyed bundling up against the frigid winds and handling the hard work. Still, he felt God had something different for him— something more.

The big meal on the farm was at noon each day, and one day

in early October Jeff came in and sat at the table, waiting for Char to bring in the food. He began to take off a layer or two of his heavy clothing and as the heat of the house warmed his body, he grew drowsy. Char talked to him, but he just mumbled responses. "We've just got to know what the Lord wants us to do," she said.

Jeff roused a bit. "We'll know by the 15th of November," he said. Naming that date surprised him as much as it did Char. He had nothing to base it on, no reason at all for saying it.

"How do you know?" Char asked.

"I don't know." Jeff wasn't into strange experiences, and he felt funny about this one. He thought maybe they should claim the date in prayer. They joined hands and prayed, taking November 15 as a promise from God.

Don Berry, personnel director of MAF, visited the Heritages in October. While there were many holes in Jeff's biblical background and schooling, Berry said there was a possibility he could qualify for the January 1975 candidate class where he could pick up some of the requirements. Jeff promised he would come to California for the class in January if he was accepted, but he insisted that he and Char be allowed to return to Ohio after that before they made any long-term commitment.

By the middle of the month Jeff had changed temporary jobs and was working for a Christian who owned heavy equipment. He enjoyed it. The man was nice and the machinery complicated—just like a helicopter. One vehicle had ten different controls, nine of which had to be activated for each maneuver. Jeff caught on quickly, and his boss promised him a raise to $7.50 an hour by the end of November.

By the second week of November, Jeff's other possibilities were falling through. The owner of the ranch he wanted in Cascade, Montana, got an offer he couldn't refuse from state developers who wanted to turn the property into a game preserve. And Jeff had soured on the crop spraying company owner after discovering things he didn't like about the man's business ethics.

So now what was he supposed to do? Give up a job he liked with a boss who liked him and money that was pretty good for a nonunion job in those days? Perhaps the job was God's answer. He knew it probably wasn't, because despite the close prayer fellowship he had with his boss and the other Christian circles he was involved in, Jeff's job held no intrinsic ministry. November 14 brought a confirming letter from Don Berry saying that MAF had approved Jeff for the January class if he wanted to come. Jeff continued to hold the option of waiting until he returned from that session before making his decision. "I wanted to keep all my options open—even though two had already disintegrated—and not take any risks." Char was ready to go, but Jeff wasn't.

The day that letter came, Jeff had an accident. He was at the controls of a Grade-All, which sits on a pivot on the back of a flatbed truck, when his foot grazed the control that held up the gigantic scooping bucket. The monster dropped straight through the roof of the empty cab of the truck and smashed it flat. "No sweat," his boss said, characteristically. "Nobody hurt; it was an accident; don't worry about it. I have insurance."

That evening at midnight Jeff was awakened by a phone call from his boss.

"Jeff," he said, "I've been on my knees since seven o'clock and I can't sleep or get any peace. All I know for sure is that the Lord doesn't want me to keep you in my employ." He assured Jeff that it had nothing to do with the accident. "Thirty days from now I might hire you back, but right now I feel led to let you go."

Jeff knew how close his boss was to the Lord. "That's all right," Jeff said. "I understand. If the Lord told you that, then that's that. I'll take it as from the Lord." But when he hung up, he still didn't know what it all meant. And the next morning he was worried. Now there was nothing to fall back on if he got to California and decided that missionary aviation was not for him. The last security blanket had been ripped from his bed.

At 7:00 A.M. he shuffled out to his pickup truck in the snow.

As it warmed up he turned the radio on low and rested his head on the steering wheel. "Lord, let us know what You want," he prayed. "We really want to know Your will. I feel that something is going on, and I want to know what it is." And then, surprising himself—for this was out of the ordinary for him—he continued praying: "Our Father, which art in heaven, hallowed be Thy name. Thy kingdom come, Thy will be done on earth as it is in heaven. Give us this day our daily bread, and forgive us our sins as we forgive those who sin against us. And lead us not into temptation, but deliver us from evil. For Thine is the kingdom, and the power, and the glory forever. Amen."

Char came out onto the porch. "Phone for you," she called out. It was November 15.

JEFF HERITAGE
November 1974—June 1976

The caller was Don Berry of MAF. Here it was, 7:30 in the morning in Ohio; that meant it was 5:30 in California where Don was calling from.

He simply wanted to know how things were going, but there was no simple way for Jeff to tell him. "Sit back," Jeff advised. Then he ran it all down, chronologically. Everything, the whole story. "I guess the Lord's trying to tell us we're supposed to go out there, Don."

Berry was intrigued and reiterated the openness of MAF to the Heritages' candidacy and their attendance at the January class. After the conversation, Jeff ambled into the front room to sit and think. Char brought him coffee and he lit a cigaret. He stared into his cup, wondering. *Okay,* he told himself, *if we move, where will we get the money?* They had less than five hundred dollars in the bank. As he lifted the coffee to his lips, his eyes fell on his treasured stereo system. *I'll sell that,* he decided without hesitation.

Jeff knew immediately that he was on the right track. If the Lord could release him from that stereo, it meant he wouldn't have trouble giving up the many other things he would have to sacrifice for this move. His favorite plaything was only the first.

Something had broken loose in him. He knew he could do it

with the Lord's help. That the Lord had seemed to make the decision so easy—though sacrificial—gave him real confidence. The 44-foot housetrailer Jeff had planned to convert to a helicopter carrier was quickly rebuilt into a 20-foot trailer that would carry all his and Char's belongings. A month and two days after the phone call, they left Ohio—in a snowstorm—destination Tacoma, Washington, for Christmas; then on to Fullerton, California.

Had Jeff or any MAF personnel realized how dramatically strategic the helicopter would be in the jungles of one of the last mission frontiers, they might not have been surprised at the stepped-up Satanic attack upon Jeff and Char Heritage. All Christians are opposed by the powers of darkness, of course, but—as Jeff readily admits—he was the weak link in the MAF chain, and that's where the real stress was concentrated.

That Jeff would eventually make it to Irian Jaya—just in time for the most monumental disaster in the island's history—proved that God was in the battle too. While the Heritages went through more than what one young couple and by now three little sons should have to endure, the Spirit of the Lord was with them. "You don't pull a 20-foot trailer through three blizzards across the northern United States in the dead of winter without a scratch unless Someone is watching out for you," Jeff says.

Reaching Fullerton via Tacoma by January 6, Jeff began getting the impression that God had him on a crash course to prepare him for the mission field; and Jeff wasn't entirely sure yet that he wanted to go. Things had happened so fast. It seemed as if he and Char were following God's will, but how could he know for sure? Candidacy was not a major problem, though Jeff began working in earnest to quit smoking. He and Char were accepted by MAF, and a very difficult year began. They felt as if they were growing spiritually, but the testing had just started.

First, Jeff had to leave the family in Tacoma for three months while he took his helicopter orientation through JAARS (MAF had no such program at the time). Being away from his family got old quickly, and Jeff's faith was not yet strong enough to cope with it. The separation left him strangely affected, even when he was reunited with them. Discouraged, he began working with MAF people to get acquainted and become oriented to what teamwork on the field would entail.

It wasn't working. Jeff was cracking. His schedule was demanding, the studies grueling. His gung-ho personality grated on other candidates and the training, deputation, and pressure were too much for him. His life had been turned upside down and he had hardly had a chance to think it through, let alone deal with it.

Most of his colleagues were lifelong Christians or even sons and daughters of missionaries (known to all and especially to each other as MKs—missionary kids). They had known all their lives that this was their destiny. Jeff was giving up all his previous goals and ambitions. Everything standard and accepted in his world had been left far behind. Things these people took in stride were things to which he had to reconcile himself.

Only later would he realize what value there was in such a grind. It forced him and Char to become a little more independent of each other—a crucial gift for the life on the field. Yet in another sense, for this young man anyway, it was too much. A year after having been accepted into candidacy by MAF, early in January of 1976, Jeff had suddenly had enough.

Just one month and three days before their scheduled departure for Indonesia, Jeff walked out of the house in Tacoma and moved in with two former army buddies. He stayed in for days at a time and was ambiguous with Don Berry of MAF. He told Char that he would just have to let her know when he found himself.

Berry was immediately skeptical about Jeff's future with the organization, of course. Char was scared to death. She thought Jeff had had a breakdown. He agrees. "I think I cracked temporarily. I was at loose ends. I wasn't cooperative with anyone who wanted to help. I didn't know what was going on myself, but I knew I didn't want help or advice right then. I wanted time to get into my own head, which was what a lot of people were saying and doing those days. It was selfish and insensitive of me, but perhaps it was the only way I could finally grow up—the hard way."

After several days, Jeff returned home. He still seemed detached and occasionally defensive, but he did agree to counseling. And he was sorry for the grief he had caused his family.

Char and Jeff's pastor said the right things at the right time, pulling no punches with Jeff and making him face up to his responsibilities. He called the cop-out just what it was and urged Jeff to become a spiritual leader in his home, to pull himself together, and leave the rest to God. The confrontation wasn't a magic cure-all, and MAF was still concerned. They required the Heritages to spend several weeks in Fullerton to be sure they were ready, and Jeff underwent regular counseling with the MAF psychologist too.

It would be years before he would speculate that much of his problem was due to his having been put on Satan's priority list because "he knew that the helicopter could penetrate right into his back pocket. We were going to go in there and leave him standing naked and losing. We would penetrate the jungles of Indonesia valley by valley where canoes and fixed-wing planes couldn't go. Satan knew he had to stop us, and he almost did. We finally left for Irian prepared to do the job, but of course we still carried a lot of problems with us."

When they arrived on the field, what Jeff and Char had been through seemed like a bad dream, as if it had happened to someone else. Surely Jeff couldn't have deserted his family and considered not following the Lord to this place. He continued to grow spiritually through fellowship with what he considered "really beautiful people [his MAF counterparts in Sentani], nice situations, and bad situations."

One of the bad situations was not being able to fly right away—the toughest adjustment for any newcomer after working, training, planning, studying, and raising support for up to two years. He gets to the field, adjusts to the new time zone, and then expects to jump into the cockpit. But there is often thirty or forty days' worth of red tape in getting permissions and licenses and certifications.

The helicopter was so new that it had not yet been approved by government officials from Jakarta. [MAF has begun preparing candidates for such delays. To avoid early frustration beyond the usual adjustments to a foreign setting, MAF warns new pilots that it could be as long as four to six weeks after their arrival on the field before they will actually pilot a plane.]

Knowing his tendency toward being too intense, Jeff attempted to come off low-key, but the stance was unnatural and backfired into personality clashes. But he learned and grew quickly under the forgiving hand of his colleagues, who were compassionate and who encouraged him in his strengths: enthusiasm and a willingness to work hard.

He worked through his problems and developed good working relationships. Soon he had no enemies. He realized that he respected and admired everyone he worked with. While no situation is ideal, Jeff Heritage quickly fell in love with his work and his new friends.

His job, which finally began in earnest when the red tape was cleared away nearly two months after his arrival, was unlike that of any other MAF pilot. The helicopter burns more fuel than the fixed-wing craft and is thus not efficient for the daily delivery and pickup runs of the Cessnas and similar planes. But it has other unique characteristics that would soon make it indispensable. The plan of Irian Program Manager Dennis Stuessi was to test the craft and the pilot and then experiment to determine where they could best be used.

Jeff flew to several mission stations to exhibit the strengths, versatility, and capabilities of the helicopter. His first task was to carry interior a 700-pound printer's camera for Wycliffe's

Summer Institute of Linguistics staff. It had been rusting in a shack on a river bank for a year because moving it inland through the jungle would have damaged the delicate mechanism. Jeff airlifted it in a sling and swung it to the base in five minutes. The SIL personnel were ecstatic at having a modern piece of machinery at a jungle outpost. They could run it by generator. It was too good to be true.

Next Jeff surveyed the entire area of operation for a missionary under the Regions Beyond Missionary Union. He staked out three landing strips in three days—which would have taken nearly two months any other way. Jeff had to learn to use surveying equipment because he was more than a pilot now. There was precious little staff to do the manual labor once he had scoped out an area. Later he would send strip reports to Sentani, and when they were followed by the local missionary's request for a first landing and inspection by a fixed-wing pilot, the chief pilot would fly in for a strip check.

Building landing strips for fixed-wing craft anywhere in the jungle is difficult. But the helicopter was going places the missionaries and pilots had never hoped to build strips in. The 'copter could virtually land in any clearing at a reasonable altitude, but the other planes needed landing strips. Once Jeff got in with the personnel and equipment to build the strips, it was only a matter of time. He was really getting into his work.

One day in Bokondini, where MAF was constructing some buildings, Jeff thought he would just be demonstrating the helicopter, but the demonstration helped kill a second bird with the same stone.

The lumber mill, where the carpenters were getting their lumber, was one valley and two mountain ridges away. MAF paid workers a dollar to carry two boards a day to the new compound. In less than forty minutes, the helicopter moved ten loads of fifteen boards each, getting the job done in a fraction of the manual time and at less than half the cost.

The first two months of work were exhausting and exciting for Jeff as he made a scheduled route during the week and transported VIPs (like the now late Dr. Bob Pierce, formerly of World Vision and then of The Samaritan's Purse) to various bases. Later in the week, he flew into Wamena and up to Langda for surveying.

By June 25, 1976, Jeff had been on the mission field for just a few months and had been in the air in the jungle mountains for about eight weeks. He was 150 miles interior from coastal Sentani where he and his wife and three boys—now seven, four, and two—lived on the MAF base.

He had put in a full day of flying and working, and—not unusual for this elevation and location and climate—his day ended in the early evening. At the Langda mountain base of the Netherlands Reformed Church where he was staying overnight, he chatted with missionaries Jan and Janny Louwerse for awhile after dinner. By 8:30 P.M., Jeff was ready to go to bed. Within minutes after stretching out in the guest room, he was sound asleep, out like a light, dead to the world, sawing logs, and any other cliché you can think of for a man who sleeps after working hard since dawn. Only an earthquake could have awakened him.

The Sowers

DINA COLE
June 25, 1976

It had been only moments since the earthquake had awakened Dina Cole and driven her out of her house at Bime, but the noise continued and it seemed like hours. Was she alone in this devastation? Had any other bases been affected? Would they have been aware of her plight? She couldn't begin to wonder. She had never been in the epicenter of an earthquake and didn't realize that as far away as several hundred miles, her colleagues were being awakened by the noises in the distance and the tremors that carried far beyond the damage-affected area.

The Cole house was not completely flush with the ground, despite having dropped most of the way from its pillars. There was still room for the dog to maneuver where he was trapped under the house, but he could not get out without help later. And there was a rabbit cage she would have to locate too. But for now, she could hardly see any light, just shadow, like trying to distinguish black on black. She shivered and began to feel the aches and pains that would be her reminder of this night for the next several weeks. The smell—when she stopped to think about it—was of freshly dug dirt. Her first thought now was of the local people.

She knew they would need her—need her to calm their fears

about the giant who had been moving in his sleep under the mountain for years and had now finally rolled all the way over as they had dreaded. Without having even seen the extent of the damage, Dina knew that she would be able to understand the earthquake while the tribespeople would not. "We had been there long enough and had enough background with them that they knew we had a Spirit called God and that He was strong and loved them. I wanted to remind them before they began the ritualistic slaughtering of their pigs [a crucial source of food] or anything else that would threaten their survival."

So before even trying to make contact with her husband or any other of her colleagues, Dina headed for the nearest village in her nightgown, mismatched tennies, and outsized jacket. She knew the people would be in shock at best, but she had to know they were all right and find out what they needed. Most of all they wanted and needed her.

The way was rough. Fissures and debris on the path made walking treacherous and slow. She could hardly believe what had happened to the carefully cleared paths she and Dave and others had painstakingly kept open for easy passage to and from the neighboring villages. The locals seemed to be able to walk through and over any terrain with their leatherlike feet and wide-spread toes, but for the missionary used to shoes, smooth paths were a necessity.

Carefully edging across the adjoining airstrip, strewn with rocks and branches, she was cautious to not step into the cracks in the earth that marred the runway. Dina moved slowly toward what was left of the main path to the village. She was halfway across the airstrip when the first major aftershock quickly followed the loud tremors that had been almost constant since the first jolt. Huge, centuries-old trees dropped and broke up, booming like cannon fire as their branches cracked against the ground and their massive trunks slammed down, ripping up their roots.

By now she was beyond fear. The practical sense that had served her so well for so long in the mountain jungles told her to just sit in the middle of the path. Rocks fell and rolled nearby, but she figured the best spot for her was as close to the middle of open space as she could be. She wasn't more than a couple of hundred yards from her house and the village, but as she sat in the way, she heard someone crying.

"Why are you crying?" she asked, straining to see through the darkness. [It was a stupid question, I know," Dina says. "But I just wanted to calm her, to let her know that unless she had been injured or lost a loved one, everything would be all right."] It was a tribeswoman and her tiny daughter.

"I was sleeping down by the river," the woman cried, "and now I can't find my pigs. My pigs are lost!"

To anyone but a missionary, that might sound like a petty thing to be concerned about at such a time, but to the locals, pigs are their livelihood. In that area a good, healthy, hardworking wife is worth one pig. And that's not meant to be derogatory, insensitive though it may sound. The natives' huts are quickly, if not easily, reconstructed. Their food gardens can be moved and replanted—admittedly not without difficulty, but done nonetheless.

Pigs, however, are valuable and scarce. They are food, they are money, they are an investment. A pig on four legs is a meal for several days in the future. The pig is not eaten until it has reproduced, and every ounce of it is then used for something. Everything edible is eaten, the bones are saved, the grease will keep a man warm on a cold night, and so on.

"Come," Dina said, "I'll help you with your girl and we'll go to the village until daylight." She found the rest of the tribespeople fearful and dazed, but basically all right. No one had been crushed by a falling hut, but as they looked up the hill to the largest settlement in the area—it numbered eighty-five houses—they saw it burning. A hut or two had fallen into one of the fires the locals start every morning at four o'clock or so, and now it had spread and was destroying the village. It was the only light for miles.

It was so dark the tribesmen built a fire of their own and sat with Dina away from the remaining buildings and trees. Soon Dina was anxious to get back to her own place; she had not yet seen her own buildings, and now that she had soothed the people the best she could, she wanted to get into her house and get some clothes on and try to make contact with other mission stations in the area.

She could only wonder about Dave and the Brumagins and all her friends within UFM and without, from Regions Beyond Missionary Union and the Christian and Missionary Alliance to the German Dutch Reformed and Mission Aviation Fellowship. Her first shock would come with just seeing the Bime airstrip she had crossed and the house she had fled. Until 5:30 and the first real light of the day, she was content to think that the area had endured "just a good shake." She seemed to have been hurt worse than any of the locals, and her wounds were not serious. It wouldn't be long before she would realize how fortunate she and they had been.

The Fliers

JERRY REEDER
July 1975

One of Jeff Heritage's most admired and respected new friends in Sentani was veteran missionary pilot Jerry Reeder who worked a couple of days a week flying and the rest running the radio repair shop on the base. He had been back on the field less than a year since his last furlough, and did he have stories to tell! God had been dealing with him, he was growing, and he had seen victory.

Jerry believes Satan did not like the idea of his exposing the counterfeiting device, and four times during Jerry's furlough in 1975 he had experienced what he considered direct satanic attacks. Any time he had two meetings in a church, he used the first to tell what he had learned of the secret to victorious living in Christ.

One attack occurred while he was driving home from an exciting and profitable meeting at which many people had told him that they had found victory and release through his message. He was on the Pennsylvania turnpike, praising the Lord for having given him the freedom to share fully during the meeting. He had memorized several Bible verses that day and was going over them in his mind as dusk set in.

As it grew darker and darker, Jerry began to thank the Lord for the night's opportunity. "I know I'm not ready now," he prayed silently, "but someday when You deem it the right time, I would like to have a ministry of directly counseling people in this area of spiritual warfare and helping set them free from Satan's snare."

Suddenly Jerry was invaded by a thought. "It wasn't really a voice," he recalls. "It was more like a memory coming back, but not my own."

"So you'd like to encounter a demon, would you?" his mind impressed upon him. "Well, just turn to your right and you'll see one sitting beside you." Jery's knuckles turned white on the steering wheel and his eyes were glued to the road.

"Lord," he prayed, "how should I deal with this?" The answer came in the form of immediate action. Jerry said aloud, "No! I refuse you the right to manifest yourself in visible form." He looked slowly to his right. Nothing. He's convinced that without the power of God and the courage it gave him to resist the powers, he would have seen a demon.

When Jeff met Jerry, Jerry had been in Sentani for only weeks. He had returned to the field in July of 1975, but his first assignment was again in Kalimantan, not as program manager again but filling in for a pilot home on furlough. During this half-year stint in Kalimantan, Jerry developed a tremendous backache he attributed to rolling some barrels of fuel up a river bank one day.

As the pain intensified he was forced to take himself off flying status. A doctor at the Baptist mission hospital in Serukam took X-rays and diagnosed two mild compression fractures of ver-tebrae. He doubted they were the result of the nine-year-old plane crash and even doubted they resulted from the barrel-rolling ordeal. An outside chance, he said, was tuberculosis of the spinal column, fairly common in the area.

"Do you think that's it?" Jerry wanted to know.

"No," the doctor said. "I really don't. Let's just attack it symptomatically until I get a better handle on it. Keep me posted."

The doctor prescribed vitamins and Jerry was soon trans-

ferred back to Irian and based in Sentani. He began flying
again, but the pain kept getting worse. One day, when it was
particularly excruciating, he flew from Sentani to Kouh. On the
way his muffler blew out and burned a hole in the cowling,
forcing him to stay overnight and wait for replacement parts.

His hosts, a Dutch family named DeWolf, arranged for him
to stay on the other end of their village in the empty home of a
mission family on furlough. Jerry excused himself from the
evening conversation early because he just couldn't get comfortable with the back pain. He walked to the guest house at about
8:00 P.M. and, after just a few minutes of prayer and Bible
reading, went straight to bed. He awoke in terror at about 3:00
A.M. It was that unreasonable, undefinable fear that reminded
him of his previous experiences with the enemy.

Nothing was scaring him that he could put his finger on, so he
figured the powers of Satan were trying to instill unreasonable
fear in him because of his work in exposing their strategy. He
shook in fear, sitting up and fighting for complete con-
sciousness. "Lord, protect me," he prayed. "Give me wisdom."

Because he was alone in the house, he began speaking aloud
as God gave him the courage. "Okay," he said. "I know you're
here and I just want to set the record straight. If anyone in this
room should be afraid, it's you, not me. You are unclean spirits
on a one-way road to hell and destruction from which there is
no reprieve, while I am a child of the living triune God.

"If there were any hope that you could be redeemed, I would
begin interceding for you right now, but since there's not a
scrap of evidence anywhere that this is even possible, I have no
choice but to come against you in the same way you come
against me: to destroy you. For this purpose Jesus Christ came
into the world, to destroy the works of the devil. He's still here
and doing the same thing."

Jerry said all this strictly on faith, for in himself, he was still
charged with unreasonable fear. He continued for about fifteen
minutes, saying things like: "I remind you that your king,
Satan, was defeated by my King of kings, Jesus Christ." Finally

the fear began to subside a bit and Jerry leaped to the offensive with a heavy barrage.

"I direct myself to the chief demon in this whole area," he said. "I command that you hear and that you not block off what I am saying. I know you have the power to blind men's minds to the glorious gospel of Jesus Christ as stated in Corinthians, but I claim right now the promise in Ephesians 6:10 that I am strong in the Lord and in the power of His might, and I claim for every man, woman, and child in this area the opportunity to hear the gospel with minds unhindered, unfettered, unblinded by your power. I claim for them the right to make reasonable choices based on the facts of the gospel, not confused by your power."

For another fifteen minutes Jerry charged on aggressively, cutting the spirits off at the knees. His fear was completely gone, replaced by joy in the Lord so that he went directly from challenging the spirits to praising his God. He sang a hymn and prayed, "Lord, where are our would-be tormenters now?"

He imagined sharing a chuckle with God as the Lord held them in derision who would dare come against His invincible strength as manifested in his servant. Jerry went back to sleep and when he awoke for the day at 6:00 A.M., another intruding thought hit him: "If you join us, we'll give you the power to put hexes on people."

So, they're back, Jerry thought, *but this time they're in a conciliatory mood.* He laughed aloud and said "You think that would begin to compare with the riches I have in Christ Jesus? Get out of here!" He dressed and started over to the DeWolf home when he realized his back pain was gone. He had been walking slightly stooped for months, but now he felt whole.

Even in a hard chair at breakfast, no pain. None while walking out to the plane and working on it, not even while kneeling underneath to pull the muffler and the exhaust off the craft. Beginning to climb into the cockpit, he expected pain to hit him as he lifted his leg high for the usual entrance to the Cessna. But no. The rudder pedals usually shot pain up through his spine. Not this time.

Jerry theorized that while his back pain had not been an issue in his encounter with the spirits the night before, he had wielded the power of Jesus Christ so strongly and boldly that the spirits responsible for the phony backache symptoms "just vacated. They left without even excusing themselves!"

Three months later he planned to share the story in a testimony at a village on Sentani Lake, but the night before, the pain returned. "This is satanic and I'll just resist it," he decided. But in the morning it was still there. A local pastor walked two miles to the lake with him and then they paddled a canoe out to the island village. Jerry decided that he didn't care if he did suffer spiritual opposition; he would give the testimony anyway.

Even after climbing into the canoe and paddling all that way, by the time Jerry left the boat, the pain had left him. He has never suffered it since. In his estimation, the experience validates his theory: the pain was a lie of Satan designed to impede Jerry's ministry against the powers of darkness.

So now that Jerry Reeder had aged a few years and had self-admittedly mellowed a bit, would his adventures become exclusively spiritual and psychological? Were his days of physical and aviational danger over? "I think anyone who flies in Irian lives through enough adventure to pack into three or four lifetimes," he said more than once. "Talk about basic motivations: what motivated me was the tense situation where you fought for your life. That brought me fully awake, and I enjoyed being fully awake. Unless there was a challenge, I slacked off."

There did seem to be fewer and fewer of the old type of adventures as Jerry's life went on. Two friends had been killed since Jerry had begun with MAF, and another would be gone before his next furlough. "You could say in effect that there were twelve of us out there [flying out of Sentani], and every four years, one of us got it. Those are high odds. Something to live with.

"But to me it has dignity and in the right sense I can say, 'Lord, to the task.' Humanly speaking, you couldn't pay me enough to stay out there and do that high-risk flying. But I'll do it for the Lord and I don't care how that sounds." Jerry's attitude goes back to the time when he sat projecting his life's end and decided to live out his days in an altered plan for God so he could do something that would count for eternity. It had already been a hard lifestyle and he wouldn't have minded staying home from even that third tour of duty, though he still flies Irian today. He'd already had enough adventure.

"But if I stayed home some new guy would have to go out and learn all those things I already knew. The best contribution I could make of my gifts and experience was to stay out and reinvest them. Some of my friends have gone home, quitting the mission to find greater fulfillment where they can see themselves advance vertically in a career outside MAF. I never felt short-circuited or like I was in a dead-end job. I get fulfillment not just from flying, and not just from MAF, but from spiritual ministries too."

And regardless how he felt in 1975 about how much he had mellowed and how much adventure he had already seen, there was more in store for Jerry Reeder. He would be thrown together with his new friend, Jeff Heritage, and would see things he never dreamed of. Things he would never forget.

DENNIS STUESSI
1976

In a strange way it is not unfair to say that the Mission Aviation Fellowship work in the Indonesian theater needed a shakeup. No one had an inkling how literally that would come to pass, but from Irian Jaya Program Manager Dennis Stuessi to the newest man on the field, it was obvious that MAF had simply never really had the money, machinery, or manpower to do the whole job that needed to be done.

Moving into the last quarter of the twentieth century, MAF was doing a herculean job with what they had, struggling along, short on resources. Dr. Bob Pierce had provided a Cessna 185 (Samaritan I) and the funds for a small helicopter, but Stuessi kept a bug in the ear of MAF Area Vice President Ken Simmelink in Jakarta. Stuessi flat needed more airplanes and pilots.

He had a fleet of Cessnas, light but functional craft that had been the bread and butter of the operation for years—but which were only one-third as effective as the bigger, more versatile Nomad. Stuessi also envisioned a need for more helicopters, but beyond the one recently acquired for the new man, Jeff Heritage, prospects looked dim. It wasn't a matter of MAF management being short-sighted or tight with the purse strings. It would just take time and money and strategy.

The new aircraft with all their modern technological features were considerably more expensive than what MAF now owned. Bringing on several more would necessitate a dramatic difference in the financial support base of the entire mission. And was Irian any more needy or privileged than the other MAF areas? Who knew when equipment might be available? The mission could acquire the machines, only to have Stuessi see them appropriated somewhere else in the world.

And even if MAF did acquire just the right craft for the Irian work, the governmental red tape alone could take up to a year before the Sentani staff could put it into operation. Had anyone been able to predict the major disaster that would even further tax the already stretched resources of Irian MAF, certainly no one would have predicted that the meager Sentani team would be able to rise to the occasion to meet the need. Except perhaps Stuessi himself.

It's not that there were not other optimists, possibility thinkers, men of faith on the team—in fact, now that Stuessi had been promoted to the area vice presidency in Jakarta and young Ed Robinson was the new program manager at Sentani, a we-can-do-it attitude permeated the compound. With Stuessi in '76, it was more than optimism; it was a determination he had brought with him from a military background. To him, a crisis was an opportunity, and the easy smiling, efficiency-oriented Stuessi was a favorite of the staff—in much the same way Robinson was later.

DENNIS STUESSI
1956–1976

The third child of a Christian mother who died when he was six
years old, Stuessi was raised in Beresford, South Dakota, by his
father. Dennis was the second generation descendant of Swiss
immigrants, and he enjoyed the rural life. He also enjoyed
attending the Evangelical United Brethren Church.

A dispute in the church when Dennis was about eleven drove
his father from regular attendance, but the young Stuessi
continued to sit under the solid Bible teaching and instruction.
When he was sixteen he ran across some memoirs of his mother
in an old scrapbook and was impressed that she wrote of being a
devout Christian ready to meet her God.

That experience coincided with his going to evangelistic
services at a nearby Evangelical Free Church and being under
the spiritual influence of his girlfriend's parents. He received
Christ one night that week.

The pastor of the Free church—Rev. Wallace Johnson—soon
left to take a church near Wheaton, Illinois, and shortly
afterwards, when the small-town-big-man-on-campus-scholar-
and-athlete started thinking about college, Rev. Johnson encouraged him to try Wheaton. Fresh off the farm, Dennis was in
for culture shock.

After craning his neck at the big buildings in Chicago, Dennis arrived on the west suburban Wheaton campus with his sights set on participating in three or four sports. It wasn't long into the fall of 1956 that Stuessi was banged up a little too much on the football field and cashed it in for the season, hoping to come back for basketball. Those were the golden years for basketball at Wheaton and when Dennis didn't quite have all it took to stay on the team, all his eggs rested in the baseball basket. He enjoyed four profitable years at his favorite sport.

"The real lessons at Wheaton," Dennis recalls, "were getting a good start in understanding the difficult doctrines of the faith, learning to live biblically, and especially maturing through the transition from a small high school to a college campus. It was a hard lesson at the time, but it made me grow up quickly. I respect the coaches and professors who brought me along."

Dennis had been affected by the story of the martyrdom of missionary pilot Nate Saint and the other missionaries slaughtered by the Auca Indians. Knowing that the army might allow him the opportunity to try aviation, Dennis gravitated toward the ROTC program at Wheaton.

Meanwhile, the girl he had known since grade school and who had been his girlfriend's best chum in high school was fast becoming the love of his life. Nancy, a pretty, outgoing girl, attended church college in Iowa, but by dating her during the summers and writing her during the school year, Dennis made sure their good-friend-double-date status gave way to the real thing.

Dennis graduated from Wheaton in June of 1960, married Nancy in Sioux Falls, South Dakota, in September, and then faced a two-year service obligation which began the following February. By taking flight training during his first two years, Dennis was obligating himself for another three-year tour of duty, and there were times when that looked so foreboding that he almost washed himself out of the training. But he stuck with it.

"I actually learned to jump out of a plane before I learned to fly one," he says. He had never been in a plane as a civilian, but in paratroop training he jumped from them regularly. "Probably not bad training for a future pilot," he says.

Dennis started his pilot training in the Army's "Bird Dog," essentially the same as the civilian Cessna 180. The extensive training saw him check out successfully in planes with such names as the L-20 Beaver (a single engine job about the size of MAF's standard Cessna 185 taildragger), the O-1 Bird Dog (in which he trained new pilots for a year and a half), the twin-engine Bonanza, the Queen Air, the Caribou, the Mohawk, and basic helicopter trainers.

After four years of marriage and almost as many in Army Aviation, Dennis was assigned two separate one-year tours of duty in Viet Nam. Normally, no emergency or compassion leaves were given, but after six months in Nam, Dennis petitioned his commanding officer and was allowed to return home for a few days to witness the birth of his second daughter, Dawn, who came along two years after Denise. Then it was back to the war.

Dennis remembers those two years away from the family as the roughest in his life. He had no idea the flight time he was amassing in the same types of planes used in missionary aviation was preparing him for his future ministry. He didn't know he would be returning to that part of the world again. All he knew was that he had a job to do. He was patriotic. He was gung-ho. He believed in what he was doing and he did it proudly and with enthusiasm, though he hated being away from Nancy and the girls.

The time would come later when he looked at the whole picture in retrospect and realized that there was tremendous wrong and loss in the Viet Nam War, and sometimes it still gnaws at him. But back then he was trained to do a job and he did it earnestly, the only way he knew how.

"Despite the opposition and the ridicule, we went ahead and did what our leaders felt was right. Had we finished the job correctly I believe we could have saved Cambodia from its eventual bloodbath. More than ten years have passed since then and situations change, and I've changed too. But I resolved then that as a leader, once I make up my mind, I'll see something through. A person needs to evaluate a situation, come to grips with it, handle it to the best of his ability and resources, and—as a Christian—rely upon the working of the Word of God and the Holy Spirit in his life. You ride it out. You see it through." Such hard lessons would pay off in years to come.

During his second year in Viet Nam, Dennis was twice assigned to short runs to the Philippines for various assignments. Both times he was invited by former army buddy and Wheaton friend Cliff Carlburg to visit and observe the work of MAF there.

The firsthand look confirmed in Dennis's mind that God was calling him to missionary aviation, specifically to MAF. After so many years of seeking God's best and praying with Nancy over it, he finally felt he had found the will of the Lord. He didn't know where it would lead him, and he would suffer second thoughts, false starts, and misfires, but the call would stick in his craw until he answered it completely.

After seven and a half years of military duty, Dennis thought he was ready for civilian life. Though he had just been promoted from captain to major, could have retired at half pay in his early forties, and would have been eligible for lucrative military and civilian educational opportunities, he jumped at the chance to get out.

He was discharged on the West Coast, and before he went home to the family in Sioux Falls, he visited MAF headquarters in California. Again he felt right about the plan to join MAF, but he learned that he would first have to qualify by obtaining his Airframe and Powerplant Mechanic's license so he could work on the planes besides just flying them—a requirement in the bush.

The day he got back to South Dakota a new school opened in his area, an extension of a vocational institution with an eighteen-month program for earning an A & P license. Because

Dennis had already met MAF's qualifications for Bible training through his course work at Wheaton, the A & P was the only requirement standing in the way of his candidacy.

The timing and location made the situation seem ideal, even providential. But within six months, Dennis was climbing the walls. "Something was wrong, either me or the school—probably a combination of both." It was the first class of its kind in the new school and there was no training equipment. It was poorly organized, and that was too much for a military man to put up with.

Dennis admits that he had a tough time adjusting to civilian life. "I had no idea what all those years in the military had done to me in terms of rigidity and daily schedule, discipline, and tolerance of civilians." He began questioning his call to missionary aviation and at times wondered why he had ever left active duty. He maintained his Army Reserve status and nursed the urge to join up as a regular again if all else failed. Then one night he had to wonder why he had even maintained his reserve status.

It wasn't easy adjusting to flying mundane runs in the reserves when he had been shot at in Viet Nam just a few months before. But this night he got all the excitement he wanted, and more. Flying alone back to Sioux Falls from a reserve weekend in Minneapolis/St. Paul, he was forced to fly at just 600 feet in the rain to stay under the brunt of thunderstorms and low clouds.

The plane was not instrument-equipped so he flew under visual flight navigation rules. He'd done it before. He was doing just fine. Until his engine began to lose oil pressure. He had passed an airport just fifteen minutes before, so he turned and followed a highway to try to make it back. It was too far for the crippled engine and he didn't have the power to climb to the 800-foot altitude necessary for parachuting.

When the oil pressure finally died and the engine froze up, Dennis considered putting her down on the highway—a well-lighted, four-lane affair that would have been perfect had it not been for the traffic. He spotted what appeared in the blackness to be an open field and glided down, the engine suddenly silent. There was no sound but the whoosh of the plane against the wintry air.

He hadn't even had time to be afraid, carefully manning the controls to keep the dead plane steady, hoping to guide her evenly to a relatively smooth landing in the snow field. He skimmed along the ground for several yards, ripped through a fence, narrowly missed a tree, and wound up in a small garden with an irrigation pipe rammed through the passenger seat behind him.

Miraculously, the plane did not catch fire, and while Dennis was shaken, he was not seriously hurt. He rolled from the plane and wobbled to a farmhouse where he called for help. Only then did he tremble over what might have been. In the daylight he saw that his landing pattern put him in the only even partially safe part of the field. Any earlier putdown to avoid the fence and tree and garden would have meant certain death in a gravel pit.

"The whole thing was a miracle, I guess," Dennis recalls. "You don't hear about too many successful forced landings at night."

In spite of the crash, Dennis thought seriously of rejoining the regular army, but he decided to give civilian life one more chance. If he had stayed at the school, he probably would have earned his A & P license, but he just couldn't take it anymore. He quit and applied to Northwest Orient Airlines for a jet pilot job. Many of his army buddies had gone the same route.

He wrote MAF of his plan and asked for any counsel they might offer, and the day he received his reporting date for Northwest Orient, he heard from MAF that they would waive the A & P requirement because of his age and experience.

Now he was really confused. Here was the open door to the call he had felt for years, yet he felt somewhat committed to

Northwest after all the interviewing and testing. Anyway, he and Nancy had begun to wonder if they were really the missionary type. Having been raised to believe that missionaries were special—saints with halos—they knew they didn't fit that category. In spite of their intention to serve the Lord and follow Him, Northwest Orient got the nod.

Perhaps if Dennis had gone straight to MAF without trying the commercial airline pilot job, he would always have wondered about it. He might always have wished he'd tried it. This way he got it out of his system, confirmed his fear that he would not be in his element in such a job. To an outsider it may have looked like a waste of time or a tactic to elude the call of God to a tougher life; for Dennis it was important.

One thing told him he was in the wrong place: the milk-run type of flying. Sure there was responsibility and danger of having so many lives dependent upon the pilot's skill, but so much of it was automated. He couldn't see flying the same routes month in and month out when his whole life had been dedicated to service. Serving country. Serving mankind. Serving God.

"I could never really see myself as an airline pilot, though I very much respect the men who can do it. It's the epitome of the pilot's ladder of success, especially back then when the 747s were on the horizon, along with the previously unheard-of $100,000-a-year salaries. But it was completely alien to my orientation, to my call."

By 1970, Dennis and Nancy had decided that MAF was their type of an organization, and they were ready. Peace came with the decision, which was aided by the loving counsel of Dennis's now late pastor Chuck Ritter.

After candidacy the Stuessis arrived in Indonesia in March of 1971 for language school in Bandung, then moved on to Irian in August. Within two years of his arrival in Sentani it became obvious that the same skills that led Dennis to the rank of U.S. army major would make him an able fill-in for the soon-to-be furloughed Irian program manager. Area Vice President Ken Simmelink asked Dennis to take over for a year until the end of his first term, but by the time Dennis and Nancy's first one-year furlough was due in May of 1975, Ken asked him to cut it a bit short and come back in January as full-time program manager.

Dennis had not come into MAF to be a manager but rather because he could fly and wanted to serve the Lord that way. His toughest job had been to learn from Ken what participative management is all about as opposed to the vertical management style of the military. It was a whole new ballgame to emphasize mutual respect all up and down the organizational chart, to play to people's strengths, regardless of where they fit in the hierarchy. Management, while there was someone to make the decisions, was a team effort. The president of the mission draws the same salary as any other MAF missionary with the same length of service. Dennis sees it as the biblical way of leaders being servants. And he loves it.

Settling in as program manager and getting the feel of the possibilities, Dennis peppered Ken Simmelink with requests for more equipment and pilots. He began seeing the whole perspective of Irian Jaya. He saw new opportunities for evangelism and missionary air support. Because of the potential that came with the helicopter and the emergence of the national church in a leadership role, Dennis developed an exciting vision of the total evangelization of Irian Jaya.

There were still dark corners of Satan's strongholds, but it was time for a plan of attack, a concerted effort to shed light into every nook and cranny. It was time to sharpen the focus, to see again where the real opportunities lay so MAF would be able to produce more results for the kingdom. Stuessi didn't know when or how it would all come about, but he knew what resources he needed to get the job done.

He didn't know that violence and death and destruction would be part of the price. Ironically, he wasn't even in the area when the crisis began that would strangely put into motion events that would result in the realization of his dream. A few days before, he and the family had flown Denise to school at Ukarumpa in Papua New Guinea, some three hundred miles from where the action would take place.

The Stuessis slept at the highland guesthouse of the Wycliffe Bible Translators' Summer Institute of Linguistics base. They were not awakened in the middle of the night as were their friends and colleagues in Irian, but Dennis was in for a shock upon his flight back.

ED ROBINSON
1940–1976

Ed Robinson was at Yawsikor in the south of Irian, an MAF base in flatland jungle swamps where the houses rested on three-foot pilings. Ed and his wife, Nancy, whom he had met while at flight training school at the Moody Bible Institute facility in Elizabethton, Tennessee, had served with MAF in the Philippines for a year and a half before being transferred to Irian Jaya in 1972.

For the last half of 1975 and the first half of 1976 they had been stationed at Yawsikor where Ed handled the one-man floatplane operation, piloting a small Cessna 185 on floats. He had been transferred to Sentani in May of '76 to give flight assistance and to serve as backup man in the accounting department. His wife and young son had settled into their quarters in Sentani by the time Ed had to shuttle back to Yawsikor to orient and check out the family that had transferred in to take his place.

Only a novice in mission aviation work wouldn't have heard of Ed's father, Paul. During World War II, not long after Ed—the second of his three sons—was born, Paul Robinson dreamed of going to Brazil as a missionary. He was pastoring a church and trying to think of ways to achieve his goal when Pearl Harbor was attacked, postponing everyone's plans. Paul learned to fly a

Piper Cub during the war years and he enjoyed it, but by the time the war was over, his family was growing and he was older than most mission boards like. His vision was to make use of small aircraft on the mission field, but there seemed nowhere to go with his idea.

Still the more he thought about it, the better it sounded. Convinced it was of the Lord, he armed himself with enthusiasm and documentation and presented the idea to the board of directors of the Moody Bible Institute in Chicago. It struck a responsive chord with the men, and one even offered to buy the first two planes. By the late 1940s, MBI had opened a flight school in Elmhurst, Illinois, and Paul Robinson became the first director.

The school would be moved first to Wooddale Airport a few miles away in the early 1950s, and then to Tennessee in the late '60s, and it would always be known for its high standards of excellence and its strict and careful preparation of pilots. They were required to learn not only to fly the plane, but also to tear it apart and reassemble it if necessary. On the mission field, it too often becomes necessary. The Moody flight school trains more mission pilots than any other school and is known worldwide as a leader in safety and a pioneer in technical advancements.

Paul Robinson's occupation made for an interesting childhood for Ed. He grew up in the Chicago area and spent a lot of time at the Elmhurst and then Wooddale airports where all the fledgling pilots and mechanics knew "Little Ed, Paul's boy."

"Everyone would say, 'Oh, you're Paul's son, and you're going to be a pilot someday, just like your dad, huh?'" Ed remembers. "As a youngster I took it the wrong way. I took it to mean that I was not a person; I was just somebody's son. I wanted to be a person in my own right and not be expected to carry on what my dad started."

Though Ed resisted any encouragement to plan for a career in mission aviation, he never doubted that he would one day be in full-time Christian service. His mother taught organ at MBI for years, and growing up in such a family made it seem natural to

Ed to pursue a Bible college education. While his father always said that he was the one of the three sons who seemed to have the aptitude for aviation, Ed pushed it from his mind until he was twenty-five years old.

His dad had soft-sold aviation to Ed all his life. "If he had come on too strong, I'm sure I never would have tried flight school, and no doubt he knew that. While I was a student at Moody just after high school, I took the battery of pre-aviation tests, mostly just to get them out of the way and to be able to say I had taken them." He scored very well on each.

After graduating from Moody and earning a degree at Michigan State University, Ed had intended to go with Greater Europe Mission and teach at their Bible institute. But while attending seminary and working in a local church, he realized that he just didn't fit. "I was too much of an outdoor type handyman. I didn't want to spend my life in the books and journals, keeping up with the latest theological debates and twists. I wanted to be on the front lines, doing the work, getting my hands dirty."

Wondering which way to turn and exactly what his niche would be, Ed at first allowed himself only the idea that he might try flight school to please his dad and to eliminate it as one of his future avenues. Since he had taken the prerequisite tests while a student at Moody, he accepted when his dad invited him to come as a special student to a flight camp that had a few openings.

If he found out it wasn't for him, he'd forget it and try something else. He would go just for the experience, the update on mission aviation, and to see how he might fit in, if at all.

Ed also had some prejudices and preconceptions about bush flying to get out of his system. He had felt for a long time that inner-city with the masses was the more valid mission service. It didn't seem to him that flying out to the jungles to work with the last lost tribes was as high a calling. "That was the way I built it in my mind, at least, to keep from having to consider it. I decided that mission aviation put a person on the fringe, the lower end of the priority scale. I wanted either to be on the front line or teach someone else to be. And to me, bush flying was not it."

Ed was a rare bird at flight camp. Here he was with a group of men, nearly all younger than he, who had dreamed all their lives of becoming missionary pilots. This was their big chance, and not all of them would make it. They would have to study and work hard and memorize and stay in shape just to survive, not to mention earning their licenses, passing the course, making the grade.

Ed had no pressure. It wasn't life and death with him. His attitude carried him through. He enjoyed the training and working with the engines and radios and flying the planes. And his mind was changed about the strategic nature of mission aviation too. "The will of God for me was that I be obedient. I came to see that mission aviation wasn't a matter of every missionary in the world flocking to the area of greatest need until that need is reduced and then suddenly flocking to the area of the next greatest need. It's more a matter of God putting in our hearts a burden for the type of individual we can reach best and the type of work we are best suited for."

As it would turn out, the shy Ed Robinson would become a favorite of his co-workers. Here was one of those rare men who listened more than he talked, and who thought before he opened his mouth. He was self-effacing, the first to pitch in and help, and never one to gossip. Never. Even his wife, Nancy, complains that he "won't even comment when I tell him something in private about someone else!" Sometimes she can tell that he agrees with her, but that's the only satisfaction she ever gets. "He can take it and take it when someone is being unfair to him," she says. "He just won't retaliate."

Well, Ed Robinson is not perfect, but his unassuming manner and diligence at his work let his management capabilities show through enough that MAF eventually named him Irian Program manager when Dennis Stuessi was moved to Jakarta as area vice-president. But that all came later.

ED ROBINSON
June 24–25, 1976

In late June of 1976, Ed and Nancy and their son were new to Sentani, and Ed was finishing up his training of Joe and Becki Hoisington back at Yawsikor.

Ed had completed his work with Joe the afternoon of June 24 and planned to leave for Sentani and his family the next morning, also transporting a couple of missionaries serving under the Regions Beyond Missionary Union. He went to bed in the guest room of the mission house that night, thinking nothing of the galvanized tank outside his bedroom window that held more than seven hundred gallons of water.

One hundred and fifty miles from the epicenter of the quake, Ed felt the first bump and awoke to hear the water sloshing in the tank. In his low-key way, he recalls thinking that "it might be wise to relocate and negotiate the next one—in the event that the first was just a foreshock—from the airstrip, away from the trees and buildings and anything else that could fall."

While he was dressing to hustle outside, the aftershock came. It was long and frightening, making the louvered windows rattle and the house quiver on its three-foot pilings. The galvanized aluminum roof made a lot of noise too. Still, Ed felt that the danger was now over, and while he didn't sleep any more, neither did he carry out his plan to head outside to the airstrip.

During the dawn flight back to Sentani he would get the full word on the disaster, and despite carrying two missionary passengers on the first leg of their trip to Australia, he would be pressed into duty at Jerry Reeder's request.

The Sowers

TERROR AT OKBAP
June 24–25, 1976

Unevangelized Fields Mission Field Leader Dave Scovill and General Missionary Jim Hively arrived at the Okbap UFM station in the highlands east of Bime on June 24. During their visit to the two missionary families headquartered there, Jim stayed in the home of Gary and Johanna Fowler and their children while Dave was the guest of Gerd and Marie Stanzsus.

The Stanzsuses are as interesting a couple as you'll find on any mission field. Though Gerd was raised in a Christian family in Hamburg, Germany, being a missionary was the last thing on his mind. Looking forward ultimately to a career as an architect, he was training to be an engineer so he could start making good money quickly. But at a missionary conference at a European Bible institute, Gerd felt called to attend Bible school.

He still wanted to be an architect, and assuming that Bible training wouldn't get in the way of his career and might even make him a more effective layman, he enrolled. He had become active in his church youth group and other activities and quickly found that his Bible study was enhancing his personal spiritual life.

Any remote possibility of going into full-time Christian work, Gerd assumed, would see him in youth work or Christian film-making. Then one night a man from the Christian and Missionary Alliance showed slides of his work in Irian Jaya to the students at the Bible school. "I don't know what happened," Gerd says. "The Lord just gave me a love for those people. I knew I had to go."

He had never thought he would be interested in such a life or even that part of the world, but after reading the book *Cannibal Valley*, there was no stopping him.

Gerd was not interested in any girls. Still he began wondering if he should plan such a career with or without a wife. After praying about it, he suddenly found himself attracted to Marie, an American girl who had been at the school two years without his having really noticed her before. They did not know each other.

The rules against fraternizing with the opposite sex were strict, but Gerd knew he didn't have time for a lot of preliminaries. It was 1966 and he was no longer a child. If this was God's woman for him, he wanted to know.

There was only one way to find out. During a conference week when each student had a specific job, Marie was working at the children's camp and Gerd was on garbage collection duty. He timed his pickup at the children's camp just right so he could run into Marie. Without amenities, he popped the question.

"How would you feel about becoming my life's partner?"

Marie was no dummy. In any other situation in any other part of the world, she would have reacted to such a rude entrée with a piece of her New York mind. But something was different here. Not overwhelmed with Gerd as he was with her, she was cautious in stalling for time. She had to get to know him first, to spend time with him, to know what he was all about. Where, for instance, had God called him to serve?

Suddenly Gerd was more sure of the woman he felt God had chosen for him than he was of the part of the world God had called him to. He hedged. He was general, hinting at youth work or "many other areas where one could serve the Lord." In truth, he was afraid that if he said Irian Jaya, she would say she was called to Africa or some other place that didn't jibe and that would be the end of his love at first sight.

Finally she forced the question. "You have a call to serve the Lord. Where?"

"Irian Jaya," he said.

It hit her hard. She responded slowly. "That is exactly where I have been called."

Still Marie was not ready for a whirlwind courtship. She returned to the United States for several months, during which she and Gerd corresponded often. Then they were reunited and spent much time together, getting to know each other and prayerfully seeking God's will for their future. By 1971 they were married and had begun deputation work; a year later they were in Irian Jaya under UFM.

Gerd is involved in church planting, seminars, teaching, training workers, and meeting the needs of the national church. He has learned much about the Ketenbang people in his years on the field and found them fascinating, though often difficult to work with. Up to late June 1976, his work had been exciting and challenging, and he and Marie and their children had endured a lot of thrills and trials, but none like they would face in the pre-dawn, June 25.

The Stanzsuses' house, where Gerd and Marie and their daughters, Karin and Kerstin, hosted Dave Scovill, rests on the slant of the mountainside with one corner thirteen feet off the ground on a stilt. The beautiful rock pilings Gerd had added for beauty the day before were the first things to go when the ground gave way and the racket of the crunching stones woke the entire household.

"We didn't know what was going on," Gerd recalls in his thick German accent. "We were confused by all the noise. First the rocks I had piled came down; then it seemed as if the whole mountain was going to crash in on us. I knew it was an earthquake, but past that, it was hard to think; to decide what to do, where to go; to remember which room the children had shared to make room for Dave. We couldn't even get out of bed, it was rocking so. It was as if we were on an ocean liner in a bad storm—the room rocked and swayed and the bed went up and down."

Finally Gerd and Marie tumbled from their bed onto the rippling floor, grabbed flashlights, and staggered down the tilting hallway to snatch their daughters and get outside. It amazed Gerd that the house could sway so much without falling off its stilts. Had it been made of anything but wood frame, it would have collapsed immediately.

Marie, a light sleeper, had awakened with the first slight jolt and assumed it would be just like all the other tremors they had felt since coming to the field. But it was not. "The terrible rumbling sounded as if the whole world was shaking," she says. "The children were the only things on my mind.

"Then as the quake intensified, I was convinced that the house would fall apart and we would go with it. I carried the youngest [then two years old] out and over the rock barefoot, stumbling as I went. I fell on the rocks and was amazed that she didn't cry. It was as if she knew this was something terrible and that I was doing the best I could and that she would not help by fussing about it."

The quake lasted eight minutes and the aftershocks were steady for about another ten minutes. Then they continued regularly for hours and even days, but the moments after the initial tremor and the two subsequent hard shocks were the most frightening. Marie was convinced that the whole mountain would crumble and cover them. Clutching her baby and feeling very alone (even though Gerd was hollering for Dave Scovill to get out and the Fowlers and Jim Hively were nearby), Marie grew frantic.

The scariest part was fully expecting to die and not being able to see what was causing all the noise. Whatever sounded like huge rocks hurtling down the mountainside could also be the death instrument. She bore a dull, fatalistic, helpless fear of the unknown.

She was so sure that the landslide would engulf her and her family that she ran down the valley in the darkness. No one saw her leave, and as she bounded on with her daughter in her arms, she came to her senses. "I asked myself just where I thought I was going where a landslide couldn't catch me." She turned and ran back up to where Gerd was now standing with Dave Scovill and trying to pray, his voice choked with emotion and his words hardly audible against the cracking and crashing.

Dave Scovill had known immediately that the movement and the falling rock and the roar meant earthquake and that he had to locate his flashlight and get outside. But when he reached for his light and knocked it to the floor, he crawled after it and knocked over a lamp. Deciding to just get out and forget the flashlight, he tried to stand on the shifting floor and struggle to the door. But the door wasn't where it was supposed to be. He had still not awakened enough to realize that he was in a strange house.

He felt along the wall for the door, found it, opened it, and hurried through. Right into the closet. Just as he was spinning around to come back out and find the real door, a gigantic landslide convinced everyone that the mountain was coming down. Dave fell to the floor near two oil drums and fanned a scant flare of hope that they might keep some of the timber from flattening him when the house caved in. He was convinced it was his time to die.

"I wasn't really scared. I just figured I'd had it, and I committed myself to God. I said, 'OK, Lord, I'm ready to go.' It was then that I recognized that the drums meant I was in the Stanzsus home and remembered which wall the door was on. When the noise let up for an instant I jumped up and ran outside where I saw Gerd with one of his daughters. He had called for me, but I had hardly heard."

Gerd was repeating the name of the Lord in English, not knowing what else to say. Scovill recalls that Gerd then lapsed into his native German in an earnest prayer. "I wasn't scared either," Gerd says; "just confused and frustrated in the darkness, concerned for my family and for the people we had been ministering to in the area.

"There was nothing we could do but stand around in the darkness, waiting to see if we would live or die, if the mountain would come loose and kill us or if we would somehow miraculously be spared." Finally Gerd broke into sobs.

When the house stopped shaking, the Stanzsuses and Scovill went in to find that the Fowlers and Jim Hively had dashed in there from their own home, for some reason thinking it was safer. With the first aftershock the house again swiveled on its pilings, and everyone scrambled out into the open once more. There they heard Johanna Fowler's terrifying story of racing to her baby's room and not being able to locate the crib at first because it had been slung to the other side of the room.

Every time there was a lull in the action, Gerd dashed into the house to gather a few necessities. The first time he had to rush right back out when another aftershock shook the timbers yet again. In three more trips he was finally able to put his hands on a kerosene lamp—which helped the survivors see more than they wanted to. The house was a shambles, the kitchen a disaster. The men dragged out chairs so everyone could sit in the open and await the dawn.

"Our main concern at that point, since we were all safe," Gerd says, "was the village directly below us. They were in direct line of the slide." A local who had overnighted in his garden between the mission station and his village in the valley called out to the missionaries in the pre-dawn and was thrilled to hear that they had survived. This touched the Stanzsuses, and they would be similarly moved later when many villagers checked in on them and expressed happiness that they were all right. The couple was just three weeks from furlough, and it wouldn't come soon enough.

AFTERSHOCK AT EIPOMEK
June 25, 1976

When daylight broke at Eipomek, Dave Cole and Dave and
Rick Brumagin agreed to get down to the strip and try the radio
to see how Dina at Bime and their friends at other stations had
made out. While Cole was trying to raise Dina on the radio,
Brumagin and his son quickly surveyed the area, fearing the
worst about the village below. They had heard screams and
excited talk from there for the last hour.

Later they would find that most of the people had already
been out of their huts when the first roar started, and they had
been able to run to safety. But they weren't completely safe yet,
though the initial shock of the earthquake was over. The
aftershocks and continuous landslides had just begun.

Suddenly, at the top of the hill where Dolly and Karen waited
in the tent, a terrific dam of debris and mud that had closed the
river behind them broke loose and ignited a landslide that
dragged all the vegetation and loose rock from the mountain to
the left of the tent.

The dust billowed, blocking the view of the two men and the
youth below. As Dave Cole tried in vain to reach Dina, Dave
and Rick Brumagin ran without a word up the treacherous and
exhausting hill toward where the tent had been. They gasped
and panted and peeled their eyes to see through the rising mist

and dust, hoping against hope to spot the tent still intact, miraculously unscathed. But there wasn't a doubt in either of their minds that it had been crushed by the landslide and carried down the mountain.

Dave Brumagin fought back tears as he charged up the hill, slipping and stumbling and sucking for wind. He had been so sure that leaving Dolly and Karen on high ground was safest. Now he wondered if he could dig through the rubble to rescue his wife and daughter. He wondered what life would be like without them. He wondered if his son was thinking the same things. He wondered if he should say anything or just keep running. Rick struggled to keep up with his taller, stronger dad.

Dave kept running. His chest was heavy, his throat tight. A terrible fear of life without half his family forced his mind to cry "why?" in silence with every step.

Did he really want to reach the tent location? Did he really want Rick with him right then? His head was clear but the questions plagued him. As he sought his God for strength to keep moving, the dust cleared slightly.

He saw the tent. Untouched. And the tears came.

The landslide had missed Dolly and Karen Brumagin and careened to a village below. Dave peered down at what might have happened to his wife and daughter. Three or four huts were still visible. The rest were buried or swept away. He knew people had been killed and he praised the Lord later when he learned that the toll had been just four.

It could have been so much worse, but the people had been out of their huts and scampered to safety with the sound of the slide. The swing bridges had been knocked out, the rivers blocked, and the area devastated.

Catching his first glimpse of what to this day amazes the veteran missionaries and pilots of the area, Dave Brumagin stared at bare mountains that had been covered with trees, brush, bushes, grass and all sorts of foliage and soil. It was as if the entire mountain range had been to the barber. [Years later, the fuzz of new growth has just begun.]

Dolly and Karen had heard the roar of the fateful landslide but did not realize how close it had been. They had seen that the mountains were bare and their airstrip covered, but when the landslide went by they were just waiting out the tremors. The earth was no longer in constant motion, but the regular tremors seemed as if they would never stop.

Dave and Rick were trembling as they reached the tent to sit with Dolly and Karen. The running and the wasted grief had washed over them and drained every ounce of reserve energy. Soon the whole family made its way down to the radio to see how Dave Cole was doing in his attempt to reach Dina.

First Reports

BIME
June 25, 1976

Within almost an hour of the earthquake, the sun began to peek through the mist and dirty haze of Irian Jaya. Hardly anyone within 200 miles of the epicenter was still sleeping. All were either waiting to take off in airplanes, get on the radio to see what had happened, or—as in the case of those whose stories we are following—simply to see if the destruction was as horrible as the sounds they'd heard in the darkness.

In every case, it was.

"I was just amazed as I looked around," says Dina Cole, who returned to her home in Bime from the neighboring village at about 5:30 A.M. "Our airstrip was unusable, split in many places and strewn with debris. Any building that had been constructed on the ground had collapsed. Anything on stilts had fallen over."

The house she had escaped had slid ten feet away from its moorings and several feet down. The flowers that had been near her front porch the day before were now under her dining room window. The house still quivered from time to time, and Dina heard breaking glass from inside. The househelper rescued the dog from the open space beneath the house that had originally been large enough for Dave Cole to work in. Dina ordered the househelper not to go inside the house under any circumstances, yet she herself went in briefly for some clothes and food.

"I just couldn't believe my eyes," she says. "It looked like a cyclone had hit. Everything was upside down—the furniture and the floors askew. Not one tiny segment of the home or furnishings was in its original place. It was as if someone had picked up the house and shaken it around. I wondered how I had ever gotten out."

The landslides had done most of the damage in the area, and as far as Dina could see, parts of villages had been washed away. She began to ache for the people of the region and wondered how all the work she and her family and friends had put into the various pathways could all have been destroyed by a few seconds of trembling earth—trembling that resulted in landslides that continued for days.

Dina knew she had to try to make radio contact with someone, so with the aid of her househelper and yardhelper—both Christians but very frightened by the quake—she lugged the apparatus outside and had them string the antenna in a tree. Before everything was even completely assembled, she was on the air, trying to reach her husband at Eipomek.

With the tremors still startling everyone every few minutes and the major shocks beginning to come at hourly intervals, Dina sat right out in the path, far from the trees and the house or anything else that could topple. She stayed on the air while removing from her feet slivers of glass she had ignored until now.

EIPOMEK
June 25, 1976

Finally getting through to Dave at Eipomek, Dina was relieved to hear that despite the destruction at his camp, he and the Brumagins were all right.

Dave went up to the Brumagins' tent to report the conversation, and he and Dave B. decided they might like some hot tea.

"There's the tea, and there's the water," Dolly told them weakly. "If you want it, you're going to have to make it yourselves."

It wasn't that she didn't want to help. She was just emotionally and physically drained to the point that she could hardly stand. "I couldn't think to do anythng," she admits. "I felt deathly sick to my stomach and had to sit down. I was too scared to cry and could hardly believe we had gone through the ordeal. With the earth destroyed all around us, all I could think of was how tiny we were and how big God was."

Dolly is still affected by the experience. The Brumagins are now stationed in Papua New Guinea in a two-story hostel, and even the shaking of the stairs as her children run up and down them causes her to jump. She'll never forget her family and Dave Cole sitting by the radio that morning of the quake, looking at her watch and praying that the earth would not shake again. But shake it did, every hour for days, then several times a day for months after that. The kids had trouble sleeping. Karen especially was frightened by every tremor and developed a nervous rash. "She just wanted those tremors to end. They are not the types of things you get used to, no matter how long they continue."

OKBAP
June 25, 1976

Impressed forever on the mind of Dave Scovill is the haunting picture of the first giant boulders he saw skipping down the mountainside as soon as the sun allowed enough light for the show. In the darkness it had sounded as if twelve- to eighteen-foot rocks were bouncing down the mountain like toy balls, and the light of day bore this out.

Scovill heard Dina Cole on the radio first, telling of sitting in the path in her makeshift clothes and of the damage to the area. Then her husband came on to tell of the events at Eipomek. That gave Dave Scovill his first inkling as to how far the destruction had spread. Marie Stanzsus and some others began to express their concern about the Kiwi station, located on a 200-foot precipice. [They would listen for hours for word from that base, only to assume that it was destroyed and their friends killed.]

When the locals in the Okbap area saw that the landslides had miraculously stopped at each edge of the airstrip, they told the missionaries that it appeared God was holding His hand upon the strip to keep it from danger. Marie made oatmeal for everybody, but with each tremor the missionaries and their children jumped to their feet. "It took a long time to finish eating," Marie recalls.

Gerd will always remember the mixture of dirt, water, rocks, and trees. Like ingredients for a cake batter, they seemed to form a thick mess of wet concrete that moved slowly down the mountains all day. He too was impressed with the reactions of the locals, who saw clearly that God had had His hand of protection on this place. The precarious mission station houses were still standing, while a giant rock at the end of the runway had diverted much of the landslide and protected the strip.

LANGDA
June 25, 1976

As the day finally dawned, Jeff Heritage and Jan Louwerse were staggered to see that whole sections of mountain had broken loose and crashed into the valleys. "I was new to Irian and especially to this area, so Jan kept pointing to different sections of the area and telling me where villages and parts of villages had been swept away. I looked down at one spot where I had once landed the helicopter next to a hut. The hut and half the village was gone, as if it had never been there."

Jeff ran back into the house and got on the radio. The first voice he heard was Dave Scovill's, but "then the entire island was going crazy. It seemed like everyone was on the air. From what I could determine from the conversations and reports, the epicenter seemed to be at the Bime and Eipomek areas in the eastern highlands. No one had heard from Kiwi, and the consensus was that they had to have felt the jolt, so if they were all right, they would be on the radio. We all agreed; they must have been wiped out. Our only hope was that their radio had been incapacitated but that the missionaries were okay."

SENTANI
June 25, 1976

Since Eipomek's airstrip was closed and Jerry Reeder had nowhere else to go, he stayed in his plane on the runway, listening to find out where he could be of help.

The lower third of the Eipomek airstrip was covered with mud. Bime was closed, according to Dina Cole, because of deep fissures in its surface as wide as six inches across. Fortunately the base at Nalca was temporarily deserted so no missionaries had been around there even to risk injury. A national was telling about villages having disappeared, people being injured, and some missing, but Jerry could not understand what he was saying about the strip so he decided not to risk trying a landing there.

The big concern was Kiwi. Every station asked the other about it. Has anyone heard? What's the news? Are their buildings down? Anyone hurt? Jerry was finally able to break in on the free-for-all discussion. Everyone wanted action, yet no one knew quite what to do or had enough authority to give orders. UFM Field Chairman Dave Scovill was at Okbap. From there he normally would have been in charge of UFM personnel, but he did not have access to planes and relief manpower. MAF Program Manager Dennis Stuessi was in Papua New

Guinea, and could not even be reached with the news of the quake.

Jerry had listened in for forty-five minutes when fellow MAFer Paul Pontier rode out on his motorcycle to see why Jerry was still sitting on the runway.

Jerry filled Paul in quickly and asked him to tell the loading boys to unload his plane of its usual building and food supplies and to replace it with helicopter fuel. He knew instinctively that the whole purpose of the new helicopter would be realized within the next few hours if someone would give the word that it should start shuttling into the earthquake area.

Jerry went by motorcycle to alert Mel Isaac, second in command at Sentani, of the emergency and to urge him to get on the radio and give administrative authority to move by helicopter into the quake-affected area. At 7:35 A.M. Jerry took off for Okbap with fuel for the helicopter. Ten minutes out, Mel Isaac came on the air and gave Jerry full authority to coordinate the emergency operation until further notice.

From his post at the radio for the first forty-five minutes in the morning, Jerry had probably gained more total knowledge of the situation than anyone in Indonesia, including those who had been involved at the various bases. It seemed like a minor matter at the time, but the move proved to be strategic as Jerry became the glue that helped keep an unraveling situation together. The relief effort alone could have been a disaster, but by jumping right into the middle of it when they did, Mission Aviation Fellowship got the ball rolling—something that could not have waited another hour without serious consequences.

Two of the first major objectives Jerry set for himself were to find out what was happening at Kiwi and to reunite the Coles. The latter would be an easy chore because they were just ten minutes apart by air. It would have to be done with the helicopter, however, since there would be no landing at the Bime strip by a fixed-wing plane. But simple as it would be, it was crucial to get on with it because Dina was alone and at least superficially injured, and the people of the area would be flocking to her for help and sympathy.

During his nearly one and one-half hour flight to Okbap, Jerry made contact with Ed Robinson, who was heading back to Sentani from the Yawsikor base with his two passengers. Ed had heard the concern about Kiwi and offered to divert over that site. Jerry had already decided to check on Kiwi himself, but with the chance that Ed might arrive first, he agreed. All over Irian Jaya, missionaries and pilots were glued to their radios, anxiously awaiting a report on the situation at Kiwi from Ed or Jerry or even Jeff Heritage in the helicopter—whichever craft arrived on the scene first.

MAFers Dave Swanson and Jerry Latimer, both working out of the Wamena base, took off together for Langda. They would deliver a drum of fuel there to Jeff for the chopper and Jerry L. would join Jeff as navigator. Being new to the area, Jeff would have more trouble than most without some help, with all the topographic damage and resulting loss of landmarks to tell him where he was.

When Ed Robinson heard that Jerry Latimer was en route to navigate for Jeff, he suggested to Reeder by radio that Jeff save time by taking off immediately and rendezvousing with Ed over Kiwi. Ed could then lead him into some strategic areas. Reeder vetoed that because he knew it would be easy for a 150-mph fixed-wing aircraft and a 75-mph helicopter to get separated, and then there could be real trouble.

Self-admitted gung-ho Heritage was eager to get to Kiwi, even though he knew from having monitored the Langda radio that both Reeder and Robinson were en route there. As soon as Latimer arrived, he and Jeff quickly fueled up the 'copter and were aloft within minutes, laboriously droning toward the supposedly buried Kiwi. If there was any way to help, the helicopter might be the only craft that could land, and the two fixed-wing craft could survey the area and recommend further measures.

KIWI
June 25, 1976

As Reeder neared Kiwi and Heritage maneuvered the 'copter over the mountains in the general area, they were startled but relieved to find little or no slide damage. At almost the same time, Robinson arrived over Kiwi, curious—as everyone was— why they had not radioed. Though the base was unscathed, surely they were close enough to the epicenter to have felt the quake. Ed reported no visible damage and buzzed low over the station and gunned his engine, a signal for Kiwi to come up on the radio.

"What's the plane overhead doing?" came the reply. When Ed informed them of the concern of their colleagues throughout the earthquake area and told them of the widespread damage, Kiwi said they had been on the air earlier in the morning because of the shock wave, but, hearing no one else, assumed everything and everyone else was okay. It being Saturday, they stayed off the air until Ed buzzed them.

It was hard for the rest of the concerned parties to understand, since Okbap had been on the air since a few minutes after the quake, and Bime and Eipomek had made contact with each other as early as dawn. Jerry Reeder discovered later that Kiwi had inadvertently disconnected the antenna from their radio before the early morning transmission.

The Giant's Havoc

June 25, 1976

While Robinson flew onto Sentani with his Australia-bound passengers—via Bime and Nalca so he could survey airstrip damage—a relieved Reeder called off the helicopter and directed Heritage and Latimer to Okbap. Five minutes later Jerry overflew Kiwi himself to savor the clear sight. He would beat the slower helicopter to Okbap, but he wasn't sure he would allow it enough room to land if he put his craft at the top of the runway as usual. There was no other choice for his Cessna, however. When Jeff arrived in the 'copter at a few minutes after 9:00 A.M., he put it down in a field near the bottom of the airstrip to keep away from Jerry's plane.

All hands helped roll the fuel drums down the 22-degree incline to the helicopter where Jeff fueled up again and took on some reserve. Reeder's plane was reloaded with Jim Hively's gear. Jerry lost some time conversing with the missionaries and their families, so he and Jim did not take off for Nalca until 10:35 A.M. On the way, after he told Hively of having been simply awakened by the tremor that reached Sentani, Jerry listened to Jim's story of having been jolted awake in the Fowler home by his bed banging up and down on the floor like a bucking bronco.

From the air, the Bime landmark is a ridge that juts out from the mountain and drops abruptly. As Jerry and Jim neared it just to the north, they noticed a severe landslide area, but when Jerry rounded the corner, he was shocked. Jim was speechless. Jerry got on the radio and provided a feverish description of an incredible natural phenomenon, a play-by-play that is remembered to this day by missionaries and pilots from all over the island. More than half the hills had been turned into muddy landslides, whereas in the past only a small percentage were given to slides.

Below the ridges, all Jerry and Jim could see was brown. No green at all. It was hard for anyone who had ever flown in the area—and that included all those who were listening to Jerry's transmission that morning—to even fathom a view from the air that was not the usual 95 percent green from the dense foliage on the hills, mountains, and valleys, and just 5 percent brown from the muddy river and few bare spots where food gardens had been cleared.

It was so unlike Irian that Jerry compared it to flying over Arizona desert—stone, sand, and mud everywhere. Dozens of flash floods raced down the ravines, breaking loose every few minutes and taking everything in their paths. River courses changed, were blocked, broke loose, and took off in other directions. Monstrous waves of debris and water crashed down mountainsides and high up the canyon walls before turning and heading another way.

Over the next ridge Jerry saw strips of green between strips of brown. At the ends of the brown strips that led to the river were the remains of huts and outbuildings that had slid all the way down the mountains. Jerry flew up a few long valleys toward the high ranges, drawn to them by the fascination of destruction. He said it was "like looking into the bowl of an enormous cement mixer just before the cement, gravel, and water started to mix. Tidal waves careened off canyon walls like bobsleds." Jim Hively would later call it "indescribable destruction."

In the helicopter, Jeff and Jerry Latimer listened to Jerry

Reeder's description and flew over much of the same area at the same time. "To me, the wall of water moving down the valley," Jeff says, "looked like charcoal-colored cement with the consistency of water. The landslides formed dams, and when they broke, this mixture would thunder through, ripping up trees and splitting them like so many pretzels, then scattering them into the river.

"Jerry Reeder stopped his account often because he was simply overcome. No one interrupted him. We all just listened. What could he say to people who were astonished at what they heard? A vast area of their green, lush, island was—according to this on-the-spot, live eyewitness—now simply brown. Latimer and I could attest that he was right on the money. It was all true. No exaggeration."

Heritage says the dust "billowed up like a smog on a bad day in Los Angeles. The only experience I had to compare it to was seeing the destruction following B-52 air strikes in Vietnam. They're one of the most awesome things you would ever want to see. You would follow fifteen or twenty of those planes through the lush jungle, and, where one minute there was deep, green foliage, the next minute there was nothing but craters and dirt looking like the surface of the moon. That's what the earthquake did to this stretch of mountains in Irian."

On his way back to Sentani, Ed Robinson overflew the affected area "just to get an idea of what had happened. It reminded me of the Los Angeles basin. There was a reddish smoglike haze completely uncommon to that area. We were ten thousand feet above sea level, probably six or seven thousand feet above the Bime valley, but still we could smell the freshly overturned soil through the air vents in the plane. It was just what you'd smell if a truck dumped a load of fresh wet dirt in your yard."

Reeder, Robinson and his passengers, and Heritage and Latimer all took a look at the fissures in the runway at Bime, but only Heritage and Latimer could land. There would be no putting a fixed-wing craft down on the airstrip until it could be repaired. Robinson's impression of Bime was that it looked like a green island in the middle of an ocean of brown destruction. "Just as in the path of a tornado there is often a house that is miraculously spared, here was a stretch of earth that had been affected by the earthquake, but spared by the landslides."

Ed radioed to Dina that the Bime River had been cut off and was likely forming a lake directly above her location. "You never know," he told her; "if that ever breaks, it might undermine the valley and sweep the whole business away." Dina appreciated his concern, but she wasn't ready to run. She had peace about the lake and prayed that God would let it trickle out slowly to take the pressure from it. The people needed her. There was nowhere she wanted to go.

She had told the Danis to make a huge aluminum × at the end of the runway from some of the roofing scraps on the base, to keep any planes from landing on the decimated airstrip. But when Jeff Heritage wanted to put the helicopter down there, he had to yell at her to get them to move it out of his way. The rotors would have pulled it up into the engine and caused a tragedy. "The helicopter was a new one on me," Dina admitted later. "I guess I should have known that I couldn't leave loose debris in its path."

When the way was finally clear, Jeff and Jerry Latimer landed the chopper and Jerry ran to embrace Dina. She remembers that this embarrassed Jeff a little, since she was a stranger to him and he wasn't sure just how to greet her. His first concern was to get her out of Bime, but he had a thing or two to learn about Dina Cole.

He would hardly believe it, but as she had told Ed Robinson, she wasn't about to go anywhere.

An Earthquake with a Purpose?

June 25–July 4, 1976

All Dina needed was a tent and her husband.

"I really think we should evacuate you," Jeff told her when he brought Dave. "I'm worried about the river."

"Give it another day, Jeff," she said, eyes sparkling, appreciating the drive of the young war veteran and showing off a little of her own spunk. "If no water comes through by tomorrow, then we'll worry about it too. But if we see any trickle, we should be all right."

Jeff was confused, but he could see that she would not be talked into leaving. "He probably thought we were off our rockers," Dina says, "and Dave didn't help any when he said, 'Jeff, if we don't see you again here, we'll see you up there!'"

By the time the helicopter had left the Coles alone with their local tribespeople, the day had become hot and dry. Dave and Dina's first job was to look for something to eat. The stove and refrigerator had both collapsed, and there was no drinking water. Dina scrounged up a tin of juice in the rubble from her pantry, and she and Dave shared a can of cold spaghetti. "We weren't really hungry," she says. "We were running on nerves alone."

More and more locals showed up and Dina was soon out of food. She gave them all her cookies and candies and salvageable canned goods. "Our hearts went out to the two dozen or so locals who were with us by then. We understood the quake. They didn't. We wanted to calm their fears and assure them they wouldn't starve to death. Survival is what their lives are all about."

Meanwhile, the plan to evacuate missionary families from other affected areas began. Dolly Brumagin and her children wanted out of the earthquake area as soon as possible, as did the Stanzsus and Fowler children. While the men stayed to clean up as best they could, much of the MAF work involved getting affected families out. For the next several hours—and this would continue for days—Jerry Reeder's trips interior to drop food and supplies to the locals and help fly missionaries out were highlighted by his views of the vast power of the violent eruption of nature.

"It looked like a big, science fiction movie," he says. "The topography was alive with unreal movement. Clouds of dust arose from the landslides, enormous rocks tumbled down, the Eipomek Valley was a river of mud flowing with three- to four-foot waves."

This was the kind of excitement and action that brought the mellow Jerry Reeder to full alertness. He was living—"grooving on the excitement," he says. He did not fear for the safety of his family, secure back in Sentani, and the only time he feared for his own life—and he admits enjoying the excitement of even this—came during a brief wait at Nalca when tremors that sounded like cannon shots rocked and jolted every ten minutes.

Jeff Heritage was high on the excitement of the relief operation as well. He made four or five relocations runs the first day alone, and even hovered over a dangerous ledge to lift out a member of a German research team that had been marooned in the area. Jeff knew that the helicopter had come of age on this difficult mission field in a matter of hours. He knew, as only a select few on the island knew, that the craft could go almost anywhere a helipad could be built or discovered (A small

Typical water and slide damage from the earthquake
(photo by Jerry Jenkins).

Top left: Jeff and Char Heritage and family. *Top right:* Dave Scovill (Jerry Jenkins photo). *Bottom:* Jerry and Ethel Reeder and family.

Above left: Ed and Nancy Robinson and family. *Above right:* Nancy and Dennis Stuessi. *Below:* Tiny jungle landing strip (all photos but top left by Jerry Jenkins).

Nationals of the earthquake area (photos by Jerry Jenkins).

Top row: Dave Brumagin, Dolly Brumagin, and Dave Cole. *Middle row:* The Cole house in 1978; Dina Cole. *Bottom row:* Irian girls, Marie Stanzsus, Gerd Stanzsus (photos by Jerry Jenkins).

Opposite, top: Irian nationals. The man is wearing a hunger band around his waist and a Bic pen through his nose. *Bottom:* Surveying for possible airstrip construction following the earthquake. *This page, top:* Two years after the quake, mountains remain stripped and *(right)* water is just starting to return to the riverbed (all photos but opposite bottom by Jerry Jenkins.)

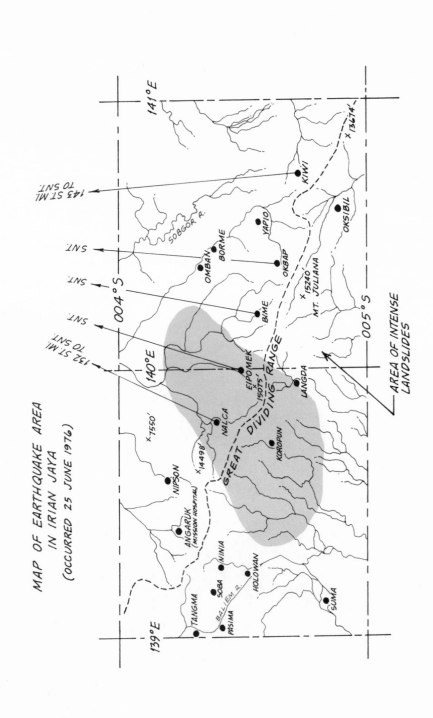

MAP OF EARTHQUAKE AREA
IN IRIAN JAYA
(OCCURRED 25 JUNE 1976)

AREA OF INTENSE
LANDSLIDES

GREAT DIVIDING RANGE

143 ST. MI. TO SNT.

132 ST. MI. TO SNT.

SNT.

SNT.

SNT.

004° S

005° S

139° E

140° E

141° E

SOBGOR R.

BALIEM R.

MT. JULIANA

× 13274'

× 5240

× 15015'

× 7550'

× 14498'

KIWI

OKSIBIL

YAPIO

OKBAP

BORME

OMBAN

BIME

EIPOMEK

LANGDA

KOROPUN

NALCA

NIPSON

ANGARUK
(MISSION HOSPITAL)

TANGMA

SOBA

NINIA

PASIMA

HOLOWAN

SUMA

clearing could serve every bit as well as a professionally hewn pad.) He began to get a vision for what all could be done in Indonesia, and Irian in particular, as the 'copter began making friends by providing relief from the quake that the fixed-winged planes could not provide.

Valleys and settlements that had never been open to the gospel would be forced to rely on the helicopter for life and would then eventually be willing to be open to the advance of the good news. It could all happen on the rotors of the helicopter, and all because God had shaken the earth for His glory.

Perhaps that was why the missionaries and pilots heard of relatively few deaths. This earthquake was a strange one because there were so few injuries. People were either killed or unharmed, and there was an incredibly small number of fatalities at that.

No, this earthquake had a purpose all its own. It was yanking mission aviation into the 1970s, and the helicopter was only the beginning. More aircraft would be needed to do the whole job, and the Indonesian government would see the need and seek to help provide many of them. Then Mission Aviation Fellowship would get to use the bigger, more versatile planes they had always dreamed of using in this ministry, but which had always been relegated to the back burner when budget time rolled around.

Other needs were always more pressing. The work had gone on successfully for so long before the addition of even the helicopter that it could surely continue. But what the MAF team would learn about the possibilities open to them with a few more of the sophisticated planes would change the face of missionary aviation in Indonesia.

Jeff Heritage saw some evacuees die the day after he had flown them out to hospitals. He saw more injuries than most of the other pilots or missionaries because the 'copter was being called on frequently to airlift victims out of places where airstrips had been covered by landslides or ripped apart by fissures. Many of the valleys had been openly hostile to the gospel and several missionaries had even been martyred attempting to reach them. Now helipads mysteriously became visible as word spread from valley to valley that the helicopter would bring food. Locals waved at Jeff and rubbed their stomachs when he rotored by.

Thousands and thousands and thousands of pounds of potatoes were dropped in dozens of flights by the 'copter and other MAF planes. Rice was no good without someone being dropped in with it to show the tribespeople how to cook it— they might eat it raw. They had no cooking utensils and had never prepared rice.

Irian Program Manager Dennis Stuessi had been with his family in Papua New Guinea at the time of the quake, dropping off his eldest daughter Denise at school. His first contacts with the Sentani base came an hour before his return landing there when he switched to the "private" MAF frequency shortly after takeoff from Wewak, the last customs check before crossing over from Papua New Guinea to Irian Jaya.

Dennis's wife, Nancy, and their two younger daughters were together in the Twin Aero Commander when Jerry Reeder came up on the radio with a full report of the earthquake at about 3:30 P.M., Monday, June 27, two and a half days after the quake. From the sound of Jerry's voice alone, Stuessi knew that this had been more than just a major tremor. It was full blown, the real thing, a schedule-impacting disaster that would affect MAF work for weeks and possibly months. He didn't realize at the time that it would actually directly affect their schedules for more than two years and would indirectly change the course of their work forever.

Stuessi was glad to have the hour to think about what he would do before facing his team of management and support personnel. "We pilots sometimes think best behind the controls of an airplane, so I had somewhat of a plan in order by the time we landed."

Jerry had frankly indicated to Dennis that he felt there was more that MAF could be doing, in spite of its usual full load of regularly scheduled flying. There were those on the team who felt it was more the government's job to provide relief for its citizens, not because they didn't want MAF to help but because they genuinely felt it was not within their realm of duties. The mission would be pressed into service by the government anyway with flights of personnel in and out of the affected areas. In addition to mission flying, MAF functions as a commercial airline in that region, being the only aviation company with small planes that fly interior. So the job of transporting government dignitaries, officials, and relief personnel would fall to them anyway.

Stuessi tended to agree with Jerry Reeder that MAF needed to take an active and vigorous role in the relief effort itself. It would be expensive and taxing, but he agreed that MAF should get its own machinery in gear and also encourage the Indonesian government to take a hard look at the situation and make it an all-out national and even international relief effort. Only MAF could provide the government an accurate picture of how things looked in the interior, and that, Stuessi felt, would spur action on the part of those individuals who could do the most good for the people. The government officials would want to come and see what the MAF men were talking about, and then diplomatic channels of relief funds would be open to get the necessary manpower and equipment to do the job.

Once the basic route of emergency food was established, a strategic survey was begun to determine exactly what was happening. How had the locals been affected? The MAF staff feared the worst, but they had to know. Their prediction was right. When the helicopter was able to get in and out of some of the valleys, the reports were ominous: the people were starving. Their gardens had been ruined. Stuessi met with MAF personnel to decide what this would mean to their schedules.

With only a few exceptions, everyone was willing to rear-

range his priorities to keep the regular runs of food and supplies
on schedule and on top of that to continue the emergency runs
of medical supplies and food to the national victims. The men
volunteered their own free time to work up to double their
normal hours in a week, to do whatever was necessary to keep
the work going, to serve the missionaries (as was their calling),
and to minister to the people in one of the few tangible ways
available to the pilots.

The missionary pilot most often centers on helping the
frontline missionaries to do their job better. Too often, there's
very little contact between the pilot and the national. But now,
the food was being delivered to the people by the pilots
themselves in many cases. They became frontline missionaries
whether that had been their calling or not. Most found it
rewarding, even exciting, though exhausting.

Most of all, they agreed that God had done two things with
the earthquake: opened up some valleys and some peoples who
had always been either indifferent or hostile toward the gospel,
and reawakened the whole field of mission aviation to the
advanced technology of the day.

Jeff Heritage felt that the difference in the spiritual attitude of
the people came via the fact that the missionary or the pilot was
now not just coming in with what the locals considered a weird
metaphysic. The missionary was not just trying to disrupt their
spiritual life and superstitions after all. He's dropping potatoes.
He's a friend. He's keeping them alive. He's offering a kind
hand. He's saving them. He's earning the right to be heard.
The people will be more likely to listen to the news of a God
who loves them now that the fact has been proven tangibly.

"I was sympathetic to that type of a role for us," Stuessi
explains, "because though I had never participated in such an
operation with MAF before, I was quite interested in it in this
case where one of the missions we support (UFM, among
others) was primarily involved. The Unevangelized Fields
Mission's frontier outreach area—the eastern highlands—was
hit the hardest, and this was the area that had been the most
resistant to the gospel.

"Make no mistake about it: while we often remind people that our pilots are not 'preaching' missionaries but missionary technicians, we know exactly why we are where we are and why we do what we do. If we didn't care about evangelism, we could be flying planes in a hundred safer places anywhere in the world and making money doing it."

Stuessi had been in Irian for six years and had agonized with UFM over their lack of penetration into the rugged terrain of some of the eastern highland strongholds of cannibalism and spirit worship. Here was the chance to make something good out of a bad situation; it was the kind of a challenge in problem-solving in the face of adversity that Dennis liked. Especially when he knew God was in it.

"Yes, I saw this as an opportunity to really meet the physical needs of the people and also to be able to minister to them spiritually."

Dennis had no idea at this point how widespread the damage or injury was. Jerry had not been able to make any accurate estimation of the number of deaths, and while the final figure shows relatively few for the size of the quake and the extent of the topographic trauma, the earliest guesses were in the thousands.

"Jerry is very responsive to human need," Dennis says. "He's very sensitive and spiritual. I look up to him as my sort of spiritual elder. He's a little older in years and in the faith, and in spite of the fact that technically he reported to me, I counted on him and looked to him for advice and counsel and guidance."

Two mornings after the intensive briefing session with his staff that included brainstorming solutions through changes in plans and procedures, Dennis Stuessi got his first personal look at the earthquake area from the air. Here it was, four full days after the initial shock and Dennis and the governor of the Regency could still see dust rising from the valleys. "Slides kept letting loose and thunderlike claps let us know that another part of a mountain had broken free. Tremors every so often during the day kept the churning and mixing and sliding and damming continuing without letup."

Some MAF personnel became a little defensive when out-
siders questioned their reports of tremors that seemed to repeat
themselves for days, but they were exonerated several weeks
later when official seismograph readings recorded two major
aftershocks and more than 1600 tremors following the earthquake itself.

Dennis was fascinated by the cascading water winding back
and forth down the valleys, seeking new paths, taking everything in its way. Such views and the realization of the terrifying
deaths some of the nationals must have suffered confirmed in
Dennis's mind that he had made the right decision to involve
MAF heavily and to encourage the Indonesian government to
take full advantage of their offerings of transportation.

Even today there are those who might be critical of the
decision, wondering if MAF should not have passed the entire
"social" responsibility on to the government or outside agencies
who specialize in such efforts. But Stuessi had seen human
suffering in his life, suffering that was not abated. He knew he
would have to commit MAF to do all that it could, serving
suffering people in the name of Jesus Christ.

"I don't deny I'm an opportunist. Here was an opportunity to
meet people's physical needs with the hope that they might be
more responsive to the gospel later." This was a region where
the tribes warred continually with each other. They were not
unified, so sharing the gospel with one group would not insure
that the entire area would embrace it. Much groundwork
needed to be laid just to get the people together, depending
upon each other, seeing each other as family. But up to this
point, there simply weren't enough missionaries to go around.
UFM was doing all it could with the personnel it had.

In fact, one of the Coles' converts, a national pastor named
Geranok, had been out preaching when the earthquake hit.
When the Coles and Geranok's family did not hear from him for
several days after the quake, they assumed him dead. Then
word came. He was out in the bush having himself a great time,
bringing people into the kingdom of God.

"I'm okay," he sent back. "I'm just taking advantage. The people are scared to death and are asking for the gospel to be preached. They're listening for the first time."

According to Jeff Heritage, a second-year Bible student from just below Nalca who missed his plane back to Mulia for his last two years of Bible school sent them word that he didn't want to come. Right after the earthquake he said, "You can't take me now. I've never had so many people come into church." Where he had had three or four people showing up on a Sunday, now over a hundred were coming every week. They drank in his messages like they would take in water in the desert.

Once Stuessi returned from his trip interior with the governor, the word on everyone's lips was *gotong-royong*, which means to work together. It's a traditional concept in Indonesia that's the same idea as when farmers or rural religious groups get together for a day and build something or finish a project for one of their members. "I wanted the governor to see the damage for three reasons," Dennis says: "First, there was no other way he could have gained a firsthand impression of it, because communication from the interior is limited. Our pilots, however, were familiar with all the devastated area. Second, I knew from everything Jerry said that it was bigger than we could handle ourselves. I felt it was the role of the government to lead the way in getting involved. And third, I knew the government would be carefully assessing our willingness to help. We would be the key to their planning, since we had the only planes capable of flying into the area."

Stuessi is convinced that the earthquake and the ensuing relief effort had both long- and short-range positive effects on MAF. Short-range, MAF became well known throughout Indonesia: "Our relationship with the government had always been good; now it was excellent. We were able to do things on short notice; things that would normally take days or weeks of red tape we were able to put together right away. The faster we met the needs of the government in the way of reports and shuttle trips of their officials into the area, the faster they turned around official clearance for things we needed. The biggest effect was the procurement of the Nomad aircraft and the Hughes helicopter, for which we needed immediate import permits—that usually took months.

"In no way do I believe that God allowed this earthquake just for us, but I do feel that His timing somehow allowed us to go through the experience. God had a hand in seeing that we got the funding we needed to lease highly expensive aircraft and buy other planes through Dr. Bob Pierce of The Samaritan's Purse and organizations such as the National Association of Evangelicals' World Relief Commission."

It had been Stuessi's goal for years to see MAF in Irian Jaya finally get enough people and machines and resources to do the job it was meant to do. "It was part of my call to management, if you will. I knew we had to gear up to do the job. We would have had to increase our fleet of Cessnas had we not acquired a Nomad. And the Hughes turbine helicopter was not something we even hoped for back then. We had projected a need for three or four Hiller helicopters, and the one we brought in for Jeff was the first of those. The many hundreds of dollars per hour of flight that were paid for our use of a Hughes during the relief operation just showed us that in spite of the cost, here was a machine that could pay for itself in a very short time. Now all we talk about are turbine this and turbine that. We're twenty years ahead of where we thought we'd be."

As with most foreign operations in a distant land, the usual course in seeking permission to acquire an expensive, sophisticated piece of equipment—especially one that might compete with something similar in the host country—is to carefully document your request, send it in to the capital, and kiss it goodbye for a year or so. But MAF contacts with the Indonesian government were so good at this time—working through their national staffer, John Karetji in Jakarta—that Director General of Civil Aviation Kardono had a personal, one-to-one, first-name relationship with him and often sought information on the relief effort.

MAF worked hard to establish and maintain this relationship with a man they respected and admired, and he was quickly able to see the necessity of their having certain equipment to keep carrying out the task of sending aid to the suffering Indonesians. His work on their behalf can hardly be calculated, according to Stuessi and Karetji. They also point to the work on their behalf by Colonel Hushiro as invaluable to their efforts.

The two words in Indonesian that mean earthquake, *Gempa Bumi*, were soon magic words. If it was needed for *Gempa Bumi*, the red tape was cut through quickly.

The governor called a strategy meeting soon after his return from the flight over the damaged area, and that's when the ball really started rolling. It was a new situation for everyone— MAF, the government, the mission agencies, and the civic groups. Thus there were bugs and problems. There are many things that Stuessi could suggest in retrospect that would have made things more efficient and smooth, but he admits that anyone at any level of any of the committees could do the same. In all, for a first-time shot at such a problem, speed was the best characteristic. The cooperation, *gotong-royong*, somehow made it all come together when tension was high and everything needed to work.

It worked so well from the government's standpoint that they worked with MAF for more than two years in rehabilitation and community development. Perhaps that seems like a long time to prolong the special relationship, but there "was never a doubt" in Dennis Stuessi's mind that "our involvement was the right thing. I felt committed to it, and I didn't want our evangelistic opportunity to be jeopardized either.

"Sure, it was a lot of bother and work and we did a lot for the government. But without their help, we wouldn't have even had the equipment to do it. Any such long-term agreement to help someone else can be strained, but under the most trying circumstances, we thank God that we came out of it with a better-than-ever relationship with the government of Indonesia."

One of the reasons the earthquake received so little global

press coverage, though it received aid from the United Nations, USAid, and many other similar organizations, was its location. "It was as if it were at the end of the world's railroad line," Stuessi says. "Even reporters who could get all the way to Sentani still had to get 135 miles inland at a time when we were restricting all except official relief personnel and cargo." MAF had the only communication network and transportation system into the area and thus received many calls for information. Almost any story that came out about the earthquake quoted MAF sources.

For nine months, MAF would transport ten thousand pounds of food every day. Stuessi pushed hard through the whole ordeal. He had decisions to make. "We were all pushing and it meant a lot to us to get the job done. There was always the friction between what choice to make. Do you cancel the missionary's supply flight in order to fly food to the earthquake area? It was a constant stab-in-the-gut type of thing. You think, *Man, I really want to help my old buddy over there today and I know he's got to get those Bible school students back to their villages, and he's going to need that kerosene.* It was only when we chartered the second Nomad from Papua New Guinea that some of the pressure was taken off."

The staff was stretched to the hilt. Regular runs were worked in as best they could. By July 4, 1976, even Program Manager Stuessi had been making flights into the earthquake area. The rule is that pilots are not to fly more than six days in a row, and every other pilot in the organization except Dennis and Mel Isaac had flown the six previous days.

So the two top administrators were on duty. With all the other pressures on him, Stuessi, at least, wasn't thrilled about it. It even put him in a touchy mood. But he was about to get a bicentennial lesson.

Action Line

July 1976

Dennis Stuessi was a long way from his homeland, but he knew that Sunday, July 4, 1976, would mark the middle or end of a three- or four-day holiday for nearly everyone in the United States. There would be parades, speeches, music, fireworks, and congratulations from all over the world on the 200th birthday of the nation.

But Dennis and Mel Isaac were flying potatoes into the earthquake-damaged spine of Irian Jaya, Indonesia. And despite having been a decorated military man, Dennis's patriotism was lost in the frustration of having to work on this day, a Sunday to boot. There was never enough time with his family, especially now that the earthquake and resultant landslides had thrown everything out of whack. He had no choice; he had made the decision to lead the way in the relief effort. He couldn't ask his staff to do something he himself wouldn't do.

So here they were. He and Mel flew over the range of rugged, jungle-covered mountains with peaks as high as 6,000 feet along the central ridge, rising to 15,240 feet at its maximum on Mount Juliana. As they reached the extremely steep high northern slopes of the main range, they were struck again by the dramatic difference in its appearance. Just ten days before, the jungle, which had formerly grown out of six- to nine-foot deep topsoil, had seemed a factory of green, a horticulturist's delight. Now all was stripped, barren.

The quality of the soil had always been poor, even in the lower slopes and valleys where the tribespeople lived. It could not support crops for long without artificial enrichment. The locals had followed the traditional slash-and-burn pattern of subsistence agriculture. This meant shifting to new food gardens regularly, first hacking away the trees (always on a steep slope so the trees would just roll away), then burning the underbrush, and leaving the ashes for fertilization.

The destruction of these gardens had been the prime disaster beyond the loss of lives. The main crops of sweet potatoes and tapioca—with some areas yielding sugar cane, sorghum, maize, bananas, and a pumpkinlike protein vegetable—were hardly grown in enough quantity to feed the people even in good weather. The locals, who shared the jungles with birds, lizards, and pigs, but little other wildlife, were generally under-nourished. When their food supplies dwindled, causing malnutrition, their hair turned red. The men wore woven belts pulled tight around their stomachs so one potato per day would make them feel full.

Anthropologists, authors, researchers, and the like might envy the people who live and work near such New Stone Age tribespeople. A quick trip in and out of the area to study the phenomenon of men and women living centuries behind the technology of the rest of the world makes it all seem a little glamorous. But it wasn't glamorous for Stuessi and Isaac that Fourth of July. In Indonesia, no one spells the "fourth" with a capital letter.

Before leaving Sentani they had removed the cargo door from the Cessna 185. Now as they buzzed as low as fifty feet off the ground over needy areas, they pushed heavy, triple-bagged sacks of food out. The pilot had to maneuver strategically for the benefit of the pusher, yet watch to be sure he didn't brush treetops or get himself too low in a canyon with no room to negotiate his way out.

After having had to buzz and push the food out at several sites, Dennis found a little airstrip interior that was open. He was tired and frustrated and dirty, but glad to be able to get out and stretch his legs at this tiny runway. He certainly wasn't up to small talk.

A government official met his plane and wished him a happy birthday. It hardly registered and Dennis wasn't in the mood to figure out what he meant. He was short with the man, trying to hide his irritation at being slowed enough to even think about the remark. "I thought he was being a bit of a wise guy, but I forced a smile and said something that maybe wasn't too kind— 'Explain yourself.'"

When the man replied that he was simply referring to the bicentennial of the United States, Dennis realized immediately that he had been genuine and was looking up to Stuessi as an American. The man's own country was a mere thirty years old and suffering growing pains. As Dennis thought about it on the return flight, he was "almost overcome with emotion. Here I was, an American, a Christian, privileged to be out here meeting the needs of people in the Third World. And there was that guy, whose country was still struggling to get on its feet and who may never have an opportunity to help someone else, greeting me while I was grumpy because I felt put upon. It woke me up."

Many MAF staffers suffered from overwork and fatigue, but they pushed on. Everyone flew record hours, way over the usual recommended limit. More than that, the continual pressure of doing the job weighed heavily on them. A missed flight or two might mean starvation for many tribespeople.

Stuessi had restricted Jerry Reeder to forty hours a month in the air because he wanted him to be in charge of the radio shack when the full-time, nonpilot radio repairman went home on furlough. Having worked as the radio man in the past when the operation was smaller, Dennis thought Jerry would be able to keep up with the radio work if he held him right at forty hours a month.

The earthquake blew that idea, and soon Jerry was putting in seventy to eighty hours of flight time a month while still trying to keep up with the radio repairs. Finally something had to give, and he was forced to let the radio work slacken.

"We all pushed ourselves beyond what we should have," Stuessi says. "There were all kinds of sacrifices, which I hesitate to call sacrifices because we gained so much from the experience. Just as our supporters have learned that they can't outgive the Lord financially, we knew that if we were doing what we were doing 'for the least of these My brethren,' we were doing it for Him.

"He made it all up to us in blessings. If we had done it in a strictly human sense for a social or economic welfare ideal, it would not have worked. We'd have grown tired too fast and probably wouldn't have been able to endure. We felt it was a ministry God had called us to. We are technically inclined people and we feel this is our gift of ministry.

"We wanted to make sure we gave as much of ourselves as the Lord allowed us to and then left a little God-room there for Him to do the miraculous. It may sound strange to hear someone say that an earthquake and landslides and an exhausting relief effort were good experiences, but I'm glad to have been a part of it."

Other people in MAF and in the EQ area were glad Stuessi was part of it too, not the least of whom was MAF Area Vice President Ken Simmelink. He had just left for his furlough to the States when the earthquake hit, and he had a tough decision to make. Should he leave his family in the U.S. [returning them would have been prohibitive] and pass up his long overdue and well-deserved break and return to bird-dog the relief operation, or find out if Program Manager Stuessi had the moxie Simmelink thought he had by letting him handle it? He chose the latter, and while Stuessi was flattered, he admits that it left three program managers sort of winging it. If it hadn't been for their commitment to make it work, things could have been worse.

The biggest problem was that the national staffer, John Karetji in Jakarta, was besieged with requests for information from the earthquake area. His reports had all come by long distance radio and infrequent phone and telegraph messages from Jayapura. Finally he was forced to ask that Dennis come to the capital city for a few days and help by at least informing him face to face of what was going on.

John had been trying to sift through the hard-to-understand and sometimes conflicting reports from various sources while fielding questions from international media people and government agencies insisting on information. Stuessi and Karetji were able to make the rounds of government agency offices and embassies together to try to paint as accurate a picture as possible of the destruction and needs in the EQ area.

Food drops averaged eight per day of 800 pounds of potatoes each, all supplied by the missions in the field, until the tenth of July. At that point the government of Indonesia took over the majority of the support need and shipped in adequate supplies of potatoes and rice. They had met a week before in Jayapura to form a central coordinating committee, which resulted in the application to the government for the assignment of a large helicopter and other heavier support aircraft to the relief operation.

Up to that time, three or four tiny Cessnas from Sentani or Wamena had picked up approximately 800 to 1,000 pounds of foodstuffs each at either Sentani or one of the interior mission stations and then dropped these at Nalca, Bime, or Eipomek, or whatever area seemed to have the most glaring immediate need. The food was then transported from these mission stations to the affected villages either by helicopter or on foot. Some stations received food drops only every third or fourth day until the government-sponsored food program helped stabilize the situation.

On July 20 a Hughes 500 from Pelita Helicopters arrived to augment the service of the Puma 'copter that had arrived earlier. Then the effort began to provide enough personnel and rice to teach the hungry people how to cook and prepare it for eating. It was a foodstuff many times easier to transport than potatoes and could make the difference between living and dying for many suffering tribes.

In a report by Jeff Heritage to Dennis Stuessi on the day-to-day earthquake relief activity of the MAF pilots, he suggested alternatives to the leasing of the $1250-per-hour Puma and listed the various crafts serving under the auspices of the Indonesian government's Central Coordinating Committee. They included: an Alouette 330 Puma helicopter, a Hughes 500C 'copter, a Hiller 12E 'copter from MAF, two MAF Cessna 185s, and a Helio Courier plane from the Summer Institute of Linguistics under the supervision of MAF.

Heritage reported that "all acquisition, warehousing, dispatching, and distribution of loads is at the direction of the Indonesian government in conjunction with civilian and governmental agencies from around the world, including UNICEF, the United States, Great Britain, Europe, and the International Red Cross."

The most ominous part of Heritage's report told of the outbreak of influenza in the entire eastern highlands region. It came at the worst possible time, and it was bad. The very area shaken by the quake was now in the throes of an epidemic.

The people associated their sickness with the change in their diet and became suspicious of the rice that was keeping them alive. In many cases they refused to eat it. "It was more likely that what made them sick," Ed Robinson says, "was what had come before. Perhaps they had contracted flu from the strangers coming in—mission personnel and government workers, the people who distributed the rice. Of course, their pure drinking water had been contaminated in many areas by the landslides, too."

Saddest of all, just when the coordinating committee and all who were cooperating felt that they had finally gotten a handle on the relief effort, the flu epidemic claimed more lives than the earthquake and landslides had. The relief effort had just barely begun meeting the needs of the people, and the schedules and routes were finally ironed out. And then this.

Outspoken Dina Cole, who had been reticent about criticizing certain outside relief agencies, finally felt that the government of Indonesia should know about abuses by some such organizations. She didn't want to jeopardize the prospect of help by anyone—and some of her colleagues cringed, hoping it wouldn't hurt the relief effort—but she was convinced that the central government had the needs of the people at heart just as she did, so she began protesting inconsistent actions every chance she got.

"Frankly, some of the agencies that came in were more of a nuisance than a help," she says. "They took out more than they brought in, and what they brought in was often malaria. They left with souvenirs, left venereal disease, ate many of the foodstuffs intended for the victims, and were simply in the way. I found the government, including the president's wife, very interested to hear this. And action was taken. We put up with some of this under normal circumstances, but I wasn't going to stand for it when people were starving to death."

Realizing that she had to do it, Dina spent much of her time entertaining visiting dignitaries and officials, though she would rather have spent the time with her people. But she weeded out the caring officials from the uncaring by challenging them to do something about the dishonest or selfish relief workers and seeing how they responded.

"One group brought in clothing," she says with a sad smile. "I told them, 'These people are not ready for clothing. You put clothes on them and think they're civilized, and I'm the one who has to stay here and scrub them down several weeks later when they still have on the same shirt and are covered with disease. If you bring clothes, bring soap. There'll come a day when they're ready for clothes, but you've got to work up to it.'

"Of course, most of the workers were nice and cooperative and sincerely wanted to help. I made sure I shared this with the government officials as well. I wanted them to know I was in

their corner and wasn't some condescending foreign know-it-all
with all the answers. I just wouldn't put up with a few groups
coming in and putting undershirts on starving children and then
taking pictures to show what progress was being made in the
relief effort.

"Sometimes they took some of these children out as orphans
when they weren't orphans at all. Perhaps I was obnoxious
about it at times, but I found the central government sympathetic to the problem and anxious to weed out the few
undesirables who are present in any large effort."

A positive result of Dina's outspokenness, she believes, is
that the government in Jakarta "now has a better idea of what it
is we missionaries do out here. It was a real eye-opener for
them, and many of them expressed their appreciation for our
giving them a firsthand view."

One of the toughest problems in fighting germs was that the
people put their dead relatives in the trees and their bones fell
to the ground after rotting in the sun for days. Dina buried
many of them, much to the consternation of the superstitious
people, but she couldn't see allowing people to die from the
diseases of their dead loved ones.

"Whole families came to us," she says, "and I'm convinced
that many of them didn't have to die. They just stopped eating.
They had the idea that once the evil spirit had them, that's it.
Why fight it? Why try to live? I told them, 'You can get better!
I've given you all the medicine and potatoes and rice and fish
[all provided by relief funds] and powdered milk (which they
preferred to eat dry)!'

"At first I spent hours mixing gallons and gallons of the
powdered milk because I was feeding about two hundred
mothers and babies and children every morning, but finally one
of the tribespeople asked why I went to all that work when they
just loved to eat it dry. It was beautiful to see their malnutri-
tion-caused red hair turn black again."

How does Dina respond when people say that she shouldn't
be feeding and helping these people socially but rather should

be giving them the gospel before they die? "That charge doesn't faze me, because Jesus said you have to feed the poor and heal the sick. He did it Himself. There is little ministry to people who are starving to death. The whole thing fits together. You can't teach them everything God has taught you unless you're living it yourself. They watch you so closely. You have to be consistent.

"These people are not stupid. Educate them and many are a lot smarter than I am. They're sharp. When we present the gospel, the Lord brings a beautiful change in their lives. What *we* do doesn't count so much. The saving work is the Lord's. And that's what it's all about."

Dennis Stuessi agrees. "We recognize that if these people become just statistics to us, something is wrong. We are here because of the Master's commission to go into all the world and to reach people for Him. Admittedly, sometimes in our professional, technical roles people become merely bodies to us, much like patients become to a busy doctor when he simply can't take the time to get personally involved with each one.

"I want my staff to be professionally precise and not let their eagerness or their enthusiasm or their emotions make them less than good pilots. But we run the danger of becoming a service unto ourselves. We must listen to the national church, hear the voices of the people, be sensitive to their needs, to their losses, to their potential."

No Rest

October 25, 1976

It would be wonderful to say that from this point, by working closely with all the missions in the area and with the central government to get on top of the relief effort, MAF made advances in cooperation and technical achievements that opened a whole new world to missionary aviation, and that was that. It's all true except that last phrase. No one can say "that was that" because the problem in an area such as Irian Jaya is that the job is never done.

No one expects it to be, but it would be nice if certain humps could be gotten over, certain barriers scaled, certain steps of progress marked. But there isn't time.

Once the flu epidemic had pretty much run its course and the landslides diminished, the dead were counted, the injured treated, the hungry started on feeding programs, food gardens were replanted, and many homeless were relocated, it could have been said that in another six months to a year the stepped-up need for hundreds of thousands of dollars and equipment and personnel would be over and things would be back to normal.

MAF would have grown in stature and capability and even vision in having made use of more expensive and versatile aircraft and proving them cost-efficient. And a book would have been written on the heroic work of normal, everyday people so Christians would be made more aware of just what the largest technical mission service agency in the world is all about.

It would have been an exciting memory for the young Jeff Heritages, the mellowed Jerry Reeders, the selfless Ed Robinsons, the wise Dennis Stuessis, the steady, loving Dina Coles, and all the others. It might have put their lives in perspective, given them something to tell their grandchildren, rounded out their spiritual and devotional lives with the knowledge that God met them in their hours of most dire need. And that would have been that.

But no.

The life of the committed Christian, particularly the missionary and mission pilot and executive, simply isn't programmed in neat little scenarios of agony and hard work followed by rewarding seasons of good feelings and senses of eternal accomplishment. Eternal rest from the labor will come, but not on this earth.

Four months to the day after the earthquake, two more frightening incidents rocked the Christians' lives and extended the relief effort alone by more than another year. It was then that they all finally recognized that there would seldom be another dull, ordinary day in their lives. They would always wonder what news the next radio transmission would bring, how severe the next tremor might be, when they could sleep through the night without wondering if the next quake would center right at their station.

Jerry Latimer was not on earthquake relief duty that late October morning. He had been assigned to return three missionary nurses to their station after a nurses' convention. The veteran pilot, who had helped Jeff Heritage by riding shotgun in the helicopter during the first couple of days of relief work, was flying a Cessna 185. When he arrived over the airstrip, he circled several times, wary of the winds that had whipped up earlier than usual.

Kent Bergsma and Ron Ludema, two other pilots, were in

another plane just a few minutes away and were monitoring Jerry's radio transmissions. Ed Robinson and Mel Isaac were also within earshot, though not close, en route to Nalca in a new Nomad. They were just beginning to feel that MAF was digging out from the avalanche of relief supplies needed in the area.

Jerry finally attempted the landing, but a downdraft hurtled him toward the ground too early and he found himself fighting the plane to keep from undershooting the end of the runway, which led down a steep cliff and into an inhabited area. He tried a pull-away at the last instant, and when Bergsma and Ludema lost radio contact, they quickly diverted to the scene. Robinson and Isaac perked up, as did everyone else near a radio at that instant.

Kent and Ron radioed the bad news. The plane had crashed into the treetops and flipped upside down to the ground where it burst into flames. They saw an inferno and black smoke, but no sign of movement or life.

One of Jerry's kids was in school thousands of miles away in Malaysia, but two younger ones were in Sentani. Dennis and Nancy Stuessi and a couple of other missionaries packed those two into the Aero Commander and headed interior. There was little hope on the glum flight. The children were silent, terrified. Their mother, at another base, had already heard the news. She was waiting for the radio report, expecting it to confirm what she feared most.

What no one knew yet was that the trees had broken the fall of the plane enough that Jerry miraculously had escaped being knocked unconscious by the impact. He had just enough time to pry the nurses' seatbelts loose and push the girl on his right out the hole where the door had been and drag the two from the backseat with him. All this was done with the four of them hanging upside down in a plane on fire.

All broke several bones, Jerry breaking a leg and an ankle and suffering burns and an injury to his back. Yet as they tumbled out of the inverted craft, they scrambled several yards to safety and collapsed, waiting for help.

Almost an hour later, personnel at the strip reported by radio that Jerry and his passengers were alive. Ed Robinson was elated. Dennis Stuessi ripped off his headphones and told Trish and Chris Latimer, "Your dad's okay! Praise the Lord!" But when he put the phones back on he heard:

"Earthquake!"

"Earthquake at Bime!"

"Earthquake!"

"Earthquake!"

Like the rings from a pebble tossed in a pond, the frantic voices of missionaries at stations on a ring from the epicenter of this new quake communicated the news. Ed Robinson sagged in his seat. "Oh, dear God, what now?"

The fatigue of the last three months hit him all at once. "I didn't have the responsibility of the whole operation at that point like Dennis did, but even from my puny perspective I sat there bawling at 180 miles an hour. What else could we do? We were stretched to capacity. The heaviness seemed more than we could bear."

Usually Ed is able to take tragedy and hardship stoically until he gets to the funeral of a friend and identifies with the loss the widow feels. "Like a doctor, you can't break down with the patient on the table." He had bit his lip when the bad and then good news about Jerry Latimer crackled over the radio. He shook his head. But another earthquake? More lives lost? More stations in the same area that would now be in need of relief? It was too much.

"It's all the more true out here that when one member suffers, we all suffer," Ed says. "With Jerry down and injured, we would all pick up the slack and do what we had to do, but it spread us thinner than we thought we could bear. I was lost in my empathy for Jerry in his pain and for his family—then wham, another earthquake. It was a left jab followed by a right cross and it just about decked me. I just wanted to roll up in a ball and die."

But he didn't. He faced it, sought God, and said, "Let's work our way out of this with His help," and he carried on. They all did: the Reeders, the Heritages, the Stuessis, the Coles, the Brumagins, the Stanzsuses, the Fowlers, the Scovills, the Hivelys, the Louwerses, the Latimers.

Who knows what will happen this week or next? It's no use their thinking about it. They have simply decided to do what they were called to do in the face of whatever is placed in their path. It will never get easier. There will be few breaks, few furloughs, infrequent times to enjoy that sense of accomplishment. And to accurately reflect their efforts, this book should never end.

It merely stops as they continue.

As this book went to press, the following information has just arrived from Charles Bennett, President of Mission Aviation Fellowship (letter dated February 17, 1981):

"On January 21, an extremely severe quake hit the island of Irian Jaya, Indonesia. It was centered in the infamous Seng Valley, site of missionary martyrdom, repentance, and now a vigorous, healthy church. It is a remote location totally dependent on MAF for all transportation. There is no semblance of a road in the entire area.

"At least 250 people are dead or missing with many injured and much damage. Their houses were destroyed. Their crops and all the topsoil in which they were planted have slid off the steep mountainsides. Even their water sources were buried. MAF responded immediately with helicopter and airplane mercy flights. First, they evacuated the injured. Then, they supplied refugees with water and food.

"Longer term, the Indonesian government may ask MAF to move some 500 to 2,000 people to another area. Meantime, these people completely depend on MAF for food and care of their injured.

"Few experiences are as personally shocking and destructive as being at the epicenter of a major earthquake. In a matter of seconds, and without warning, loved ones are killed or injured, homes and gardens destroyed, trails obliterated, and the whole future made uncertain.

"These details have just been received on MAF *helicopter*

activities in the quake zone; MAF aircraft are providing
transport from Sentani to the nearest airstrip of Holowun:

"*January 28:* Made about 17 helicopter shuttles, carrying
rice, shovels and food, plus evacuating 41 people—5 of these
medical patients. 130 people still need to be evacuated from
two villages.

"*January 29:* Flew 2 government officials to 3 villages to talk
with people about relocating. In the Seng Valley dropped 500
pounds of sweet potatoes and vegetables in forests near 3
villages. Found 14 people in forest above Sinokla and
evacuated them to Lillimahan. One of these was injured so
was flown for help. Left large sack of medicine at a village of
300 people.

"*January 30:* Dropped 2 sacks rice, made 5 shuttles,
evacuated 25 people, plus government officials who were
evacuated to Holowun.

"*February 2:* Dropped sacks rice at 4 villages. Dropped 300
pounds sweet potatoes. Evacuated 23 people. Governor
visited site on Saturday the 31st, reported continued tremors. He brought in 400 pounds sweet potatoes.

"*February 3:* Shuttles with 50 people evacuated from 4
villages. 50 known people still left in forest. Total 510 pounds
sweet potatoes dropped to 3 villages. Government doctor
flown to Lolat. 38 spades dropped at 3 villages. A team of
tribal chiefs made initial survey of new resettlement area
(Dinggala). Received report from prior survey of Koruppan
and the Solo Valleys. Will make report directly to Governor.

"*February 4:* Made 18 helicopter shuttles evacuating 97
people to Lilimahan. Government doctor flown to Lilimahan
and Sinombabuk. Government official also flown to 3 villages.
Sacks of potatoes were dropped at 3 villages. 2 shuttles were
made with 8 workers to Dinggala to prepare resettlement
site. They took in 10 axes, 10 machetes, 10 picks.

"'The dam broke at 2:00 P.M. The Suma River raised but no
damage. Received confirmation that 25 people had been
killed by earthquake at Unuklaha.'"